D1549285

Tackling Coursework

Assignments, projects, reports and
presentations

David Parker BA, MSc, PhD, CEng, MIMfg, FMS, MILog, CertEd

Dr Parker is a principal lecturer in operations management (logistics) at
Bristol Business School, University of the West of England. Prior to his current
post he was a senior lecturer in the Global Logistics and Marketing Group at
Manchester Metropolitan University. His postgraduate degrees were gained
through research, and he has lectured in higher education since 1978. He
has published extensively and undertaken numerous consultancy assignments
related to operations management and logistics.

DP Publications Ltd
Aldine Place
London W12 8AW

1994

A CIP catalogue record for this book is available from the British Library.

Copyright David Parker © 1994
ISBN 1 85805 101 0

Printed by The Guernsey Press Co. Ltd.,
Vale, Guernsey, Channel Islands

ii

Preface

Aim

The aim of this book is to give students practical guidance on how to approach and accomplish successfully the various types of course-work they will produce on a typical undergraduate business course. It would also be suitable for students at postgraduate (e.g. MBA) level, and as a preparatory text for those contemplating a research degree (e.g. MPhil).

Need

Students coming into higher education have rarely had to produce the type of work that is required of them at this level, e.g. long essays, dissertations etc. They often do not know what the difference is between essay-type assignments, reports and dissertations, or how to approach this type of work, i.e. conducting research, collecting information and presenting their results.

This is a concise guide for students, explaining the different approaches required for the different types of coursework that they will have to undertake on a regular basis to satisfy the assessment criteria for, say, a business studies degree programme.

Approach

The book is divided into chapters according to the different types of assignment: *Essays and papers, Dissertations and projects, Management reports, Seminars and presentations*. The final chapter goes into more detail on the possible research methods for any type of assignment.

The student can read the whole book in preparation for the course, or can go to the chapter that is specific to a particular assignment that has been set. The book can be used for reference and confirmation during the course. Students and lecturers will also find the marking guidelines in sections 2.4 and 2.9 of Chapter 2 and in Appendix 6 useful for assessment purposes.

At the end of the book are appendices containing details of further reading, and examples of the various types of coursework addressed in the text.

Contents

1 Introduction

This book is intended to give simple instructions on how to approach and present the various types of coursework to those starting their studies. It is not intended to restrict personal expression, but rather to emphasise that sometimes we forget the most important person when we are communicating: **the recipient of the information.**

The skills of writing scholarly pieces of work can be learned very easily. The hazards that befall students new to studying are often merely those of stylisation; that is to say, they have adequate depth of information but it has not been presented in an adequate manner. **Whilst the analysis may be adequate, it is often marred by the lack of a unifying theme or conceptual framework.**

A criticism sometimes voiced by students is that academic writing (and subsequent reading of it) is dry, boring and lacks colour. Their feelings are frequently voiced as a result of being told that their work is too journalistic, sensationalist, littered with value judgements and personal beliefs, uncorroborated by factual data and too descriptive when it should be evaluative. All these failings – and many more – can be remedied. You **can** be succinct, factual and interesting when writing papers and preparing for talks on academic subjects.

The following story illustrates an important point:

> A young reporter was continually told by his editor, 'keep to the facts.... just write the facts ... don't waffle or pad it out.' So, on the occasion when he had to report of a mother cat with her kittens on the roof of a high building, he heeded his editor's advice and endeavoured to *keep to the facts*. But thinking the piece was boring he wrote: 'Just when the mother cat's and her kittens' nine-lives appeared used, God played his hand and they jumped to safety.' On reading this his editor wrote: 'Forget the cats ... interview God!'

Over zealous use of such adjectives as: *many, large, small, massive,* plenty and huge, will be rebuked by your tutor as having no tangible measurement. Such words and phrases are meaningless, ambiguous, inaccurate and open to interpretation. In other words, you must be factual.

The body of this book will give you practical advice on some of the do's and don'ts of undertaking academic writing. It will also give you examples for discussion. Unfortunately, this does not mean that following this advice *to the letter* will ensure you a certain pass – only you can do that – but you might find it easier once you have read this book.

1.1 Fog index

An exercise that you may wish to try in order to appreciate different levels of writing is the calculation of the *Fog Index*. Put simply, this index measures a piece of writing in relation to the number of years of education needed to interpret what has been written. Assuming that education starts at five years of age, it can be assumed that for general readership an index of 10 should be aimed for. For professional reports an index of 14-15 is acceptable. Whilst this index is purely indicative, some interesting results appear when our daily newspapers are analysed. You might like to work in small groups and try the following game.

1.1.1 The newspaper exercise

I think you would agree that professional journalists are usually good at presenting information to us. Day-in-day-out they are confronted with new news breaking, the facts of which they must assimilate quickly in order to prepare a *resumé for us*. Do they think about their general readership when writing; and is there a different level of language for individual newspapers? Try the following group exercise.

Purchase a selection of daily newspapers: for example, *Daily Mirror, The Sun, The Daily Mail, Express, Daily Telegraph, The Guardian* and *The Times*. Split each newspaper into three: current affairs, regular features and the sport section. Next, apply the Fog Index (see below to see how to calculate it) to each section of each newspaper. Then answer the following questions:

- what are the Fog Indexes for each of the three sections for the *tabloids* and *broadsheet* newspapers?
- is there a pattern emerging for Fog Indexes?
- what assumptions, if any, can be drawn from your results?

For our game we shall use the classic *Gunning Fog Index,* as it is the easiest of all the indexes to apply. This can be defined as:

$$F = 0.4(A + L)$$

where: F = Fog Index

A = Average length of sentence

L = Number of long words per hundred words

Take one section of the newspaper – say, the sports section – then calculate the following:

Calculation of A

Take a sample of at least 100 sentences.

Count the words in each sentence.

Calculate the average sentence length, e.g. 28,32,34,36,29

$$A = 31.8$$

Calculation of L%

Count the number of words in your sample, i.e., those that have three or more syllables, e.g. syll-a-bles.

Then calculate the percentage, e.g. polysyllables = 16; number of words in sample = 159;

So
$$L = \frac{16}{159} \times 100$$
$$= 10\%$$

Calculation of F

Add together **A** + **L** and multiply by 0.4 to give the value of **F**. In the example here it would be:

$$(31.8 + 10) \times 0.4 = 16.72$$

General findings from playing this exercise several times reveal an interesting pattern. Do you find the same results as me? Usually I find that the index for the *current affairs* section of **all** newspapers is low. It ranges from as low as 5 up to 17; however, the tabloids are always at the lower end of the scale. Regular features have a higher index: tabloids at 7 with the broadsheets sometimes having a high of 20. Of interest, however, is the result from the sport section. There appears to be little difference between the newspapers; moreover, the index is comparatively high for all of them at 22 or above.

What can we deduce from this exercise then? It would appear that current affairs, by the very nature of being **new** information to the reader, has a low index to make it *easier* to read. Whereas the regular features can afford to be slightly more difficult due to the readership's familiarity with the material. With sport, we have a very experienced readership, and obviously there is a need for technical words and phrases to be used.

Obviously this one exercise proves little and your results may not have led you to the same conclusions as mine. So what might that tell us about research, writing and the readership? This book attempts to address these very issues of initial academic research and writing, whilst making you fully aware of readers' needs.

2 Essays and papers

2.1 Introduction

For clarity, I propose to define an *essay* or *paper* as a written response by you to a specific question posed by your tutor. Such questions are raised either to encourage you to research and write on a topic not specifically covered in lectures, or possibly to get you to probe deeper into complex issues that have previously been raised. They are therefore an important *vehicle* in your learning. As such, they are an extremely effective way of showing if you are coping with the course, and are also a means of ensuring that you appreciate the subtle and wider aspects of the topic under investigation.

Many students often never see any assignments but their own. The following advice, therefore, is concerned with writing essay-type assignments; the type of coursework that you will have to undertake on a regular basis to satisfy the assessment criteria for a Business Studies degree programme, for instance. It is intended to establish some point of reference for you.

2.2 What is required of you

You will undoubtedly have sensed a shift in responsibilities as you move from a non-degree, professional programme or school-type setting to higher education study. At school, for example, teachers tend to assume much of the responsibility for the learning that goes on. Suddenly, you now probably feel that your tutor is not giving you any guidance. She or he seems to give you very little **solid** advice. This shift in responsibility often comes as a shock to new students who are still expecting to be told what to learn, how to learn it, and to be goaded into learning it. However, there is another even more fundamental shift in responsibility which many find even harder to get used to, and this is the responsibility for deciding **what is true**.

Prior to joining your current programme, much of what was to be learned was presented as a set of facts. You got marks for the accuracy with which you could repeat back to the teacher what he or she had told you. (Of course, this is an over simplification). By contrast, the **truth** about the world is taken to be far more uncertain. Individual lecturers in your current institution are likely to present you with various and alternative ideas and theories, some of which they will favour more than others, and you are expected to come to an understanding of some of them. But you are also expected to form your **own** judgment about their strengths and weaknesses.

This has important consequences, in that you have to treat your studies as an enquiry into the nature of the world. You have to be able to consider alternative ideas, not just learn facts; you have to be able to argue the merits of one idea against another, not just list them. Thus, the whole emphasis shifts from that of being a passive recipient to being an active enquirer. This requires that you no longer await the instructions of an *all-knowing* teacher but work out your own plans for constructing sense for yourself out of the range of ideas open to you. Your ultimate goal is to achieve independence as a scholar in your own right, and although you may be given assistance while you are learning to cope, it is this independence that remains your target.

What you have to do to show adequate scholarly aptitude, is to put onto paper an answer to a specific question that demonstrates:

- ☐ relevance
- ☐ adequate research
- ☐ sound argument supported by references and data
- ☐ logical structure
- ☐ clarity
- ☐ acceptable standard of presentation

Having to express your thoughts in writing will give you a chance to think through your ideas. You will find, as you begin to write down your thoughts, that they will become much clearer and you will understand the material much more. A topic under investigation is rarely clear-cut with obvious influencing factors. Usually there are many issues, factors and agents all playing a part. The *real world* of business and commerce is never a simplistic thing to explain. What are the various theories for this topic? What different schools of thought can you detect from what you have read? Can you categorise the range of differing perspectives? Thus, in your essay you have to decide what are the important facts and theories and explain to the reader in a concise way your reasoned arguments. Not, you may think, an easy task. Perhaps not – but it should be an enjoyable challenge if you take away the mystique and chore of writing.

Instead of thinking of writing an essay as one task, it will help if you break it down into smaller stages. You will find that by following this organised approach, the work is much more enjoyable, and you will learn more of the topic under investigation.

2.3 Getting yourself organised

Never leave the assignment to the last minute. Establish what the rest of your work load is likely to be and give yourself ample time for literature searches, etc. Remember that when you eventually take up a position in business, planning and organisation are prerequisites for all good managers; so if you cannot become good at time-management now, how will you cope when you are responsible for a team of staff?

Plan your completion dates and deadlines in advance. A marked-up wall-chart (or personal diary) is essential to make sure you do not miss assignment submission dates, tutorials and so on. Ideally you should be able to work undisturbed, with space to spread your books and papers out, with easy access to files and with good lighting and heating. How close to this ideal can you get? Before you start your studying get yourself a good supply of ball point pens, A4 note pads, pocket files, file boxes, shelf space and a good dictionary. You will accumulate a great deal of printed matter, so it is vital to file it under different headings. A final piece of advice for your personal organisation: make sure your family and friends understand your study plans and know when to leave you alone. From my experience, leisure is far better enjoyed if it is planned within a study programme – you never seem to enjoy yourself as much when you know the time should be used preparing an imminent assignment. Equally, when you know that time for leisure and relaxation is part of a planned schedule, it is much more enjoyable.

2.4 Essay writing: the craft

The most difficult, the most crucial, and the one aspect of writing on which you will spend most time and effort, is the development of your *powers of written expression*. Often, essays present a rather brief and artificial kind of writing task. Nevertheless, you are not just being asked to learn tricks to satisfy an arbitrary rule system. You are being put through exercises to develop your powers of self expression. The restrictions imposed by writing tasks are intended to make you better at broader and more useful forms of writing. The cutting down of tasks within formalised limits makes it easier to coach you and to check your progress. Of course, you will have constant feedback in the form of marks and comments from your lecturers' so that you can get an idea of your progress. Apart from the intrinsic value of essay writing in developing your writing style, it also serves the very important function of helping you to learn the course material. You may feel that you understand various arguments as you read them, but your understanding inevitably becomes deeper and more firmly rooted as you attempt to manipulate the arguments for yourself.

The written assignment also provides the basis for assessing your progress with the course. To give you an idea of how these marks are applied, I thought it would be useful to show you some guidelines on how an assignment might be assessed:

70–100%: **excellent** – *hangs together* particularly well – *adopts a good line of argument* and brings it off successfully – shows *awareness* of broad and subtle *implications of issues.*

60–69%: **promising** – attacks the question confidently – *identifies* the appropriate *issues* – *uses evidence and examples well* – argues from recognised stances and *uses quotations and references where relevant,*i.e., recognisably a valid piece of analysis though perhaps lacking the poise, polish and fluency.

50–59%: **solid but rather pedestrian** – workmanlike – refers to much of the relevant handouts and generally grasps the point correctly, but uneven in structure and fails to recognise broader implications of issues; shows intelligence and application but lacks a clear grasp of the process of analysis.

40–49%: **struggling** – student appears to have difficulty in comprehending the course material and the question set – lacks skill in presenting arguments – but in patches suggests that worthwhile progress is being made.

29–39%: **not coping** – little evidence of grasp of the course material – poor approach to the question – disorganised and poorly expressed.

0–28%: **hopeless** – appears to have given little effort to understanding the course material. Either fails to realise what is required at this level or is lacking in the necessary abilities.

2.5 Approach to planning and starting your work

Assignment writing consists of three key stages:

☐ getting your main *ideas* on paper

☐ planning and researching the literature

☐ writing

I want to discuss with you how I complete these stages using an example of an essay that a typical business studies student might be asked to write. I am going to plan the essay partly in an attempt to illustrate a number of specific points about essay writing. Let us begin with what is probably the most difficult part – *how to get started.*

2.5.1 The question

Always start your planning with the question. That sounds obvious, but it is surprising how many essays seem to get written with only a vague reference to the question. It is important to read the question carefully and analyse exactly what is required of you. I guess you find it just as irritating as I do when politicians on the television refuse to answer the question put to them, or seem to be utterly oblivious of the intentions of the questioner. Exactly the same concern applies to essays. The answer that points out clearly the implications of the question and then proceeds to answer it is a pleasure to read. Evasive, vague or irrelevant types of answer are maddening. Frequently politicians know exactly what the question requires but avoid answering for their own particular motives; students do not have that kind of excuse, but sometimes have a *packaged answer* looking for the right question. We are often loath to change and edit material even if we know it is not required by the question. So let us look at my example of a question.

2.5.2 What does the question require of you?

'Docklands decline was inevitable; what happened in the area in the 60s and 70s was a reflection of national and international economic trends.' Discuss.

What does this question require us to do? Assignments are meant to make us think about a central issue in addition to considering wider implications. You are not merely being asked to show that you have read all the handouts given to you by your lecturers. Nor are you being checked-up on to see if you have read sufficient books. You are being asked to show that you can select points from the material given, and from the books you have read, which are particularly *relevant to the specific question set* and that you can argue a case around these points. Consequently a great deal rests upon your interpretation of the meaning of the question. It is only too common an experience as a student to be told that you have included irrelevant material or that your argument misses the point of the question. Always give yourself time to stop and ponder the question before plunging in.

One simple technique to help you to interpret the question is to underline the important words in the question and to satisfy yourself you are sure what each one means. Here, such words are *discuss, docklands, economic trends, national and international* and *60s and 70s.*

It is also important to make sure you understand the meaning of the *doing or directive* word. Here we are asked to *discuss,* but on other occasions we may be asked to describe, assess, evaluate, compare or contrast. Make sure you understand the implications of these words before putting pen to paper. This is not merely an academic exercise; it does matter that we can distinguish between *discuss* and *describe. Describe* requires you to give a detailed account, whereas *discuss* goes one step further – not only is it necessary to set out the detail of an event or theory, you have also to give reasons for and against the importance of the event or the relevance or plausibility of the theory. To *discuss* is more difficult than to than to *describe.* It requires you to sift evidence and to weigh up arguments.

Directive words often used in essay questions are:

Compare – Are the things similar or are there important differences? Which do you think is best? Why?

Consider – See discuss.

Contrast – Look for differences.

Criticise – Use evidence to support your opinion on the value or merit of theories, facts of others. Criticism should be positive as well as negative.

Define – Give the meaning.

Describe – Write in detail.

Differentiate – Explain the difference.

Discuss – Investigate and examine the implications. Debate the arguments for and against and possibly consider alternatives.

Explain – Make clear.

Illustrate – Give examples which make the point clear.

Interpret – Explain the meaning in your own words.

Justify – Give reasons to support an argument or action.

Outline – Choose the most important aspects of a topic. Ignore the minor detail.

Relate – Show the connection between things.

State – Write briefly the main points.

Summarise – Bring together the main points.

Trace – Show how something has developed to its current position.

Another useful technique in analysing the question is to break it up into a number of other questions. For example, we could ask: *are there processes and factors that have caused economic and social changes?*

2.5.3 Getting your ideas on paper and planning

We begin then, with the question. Once we have begun to understand what is being asked we move into the three stages identified at the start of section 2.5. I usually take the first and second stages together – that is, getting ideas down on paper and planning. I draw a line down the middle of the page and on the left-hand side I put all the concepts, phrases or odd notes which I think might be important, and on the right-hand side I organise them. My rough draft can be seen in Figure 2.1.

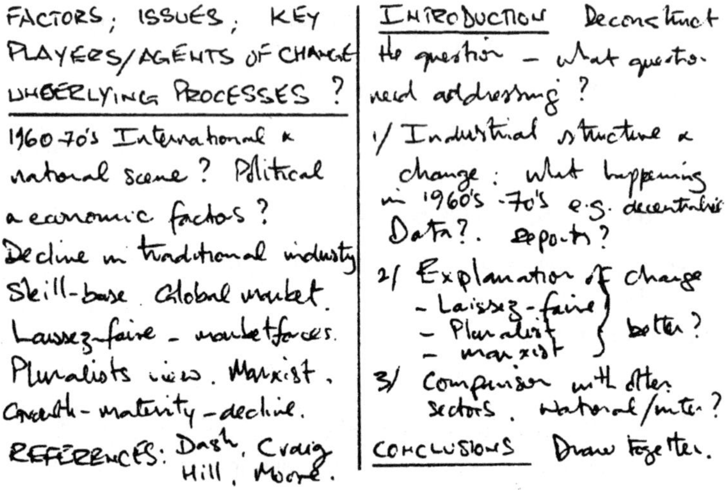

FACTORS; ISSUES; KEY PLAYERS/AGENTS OF CHANGE UNDERLYING PROCESSES ?

1960-70's International & national scene? Political & economic factors? Decline in traditional industry Skill-base. Global market. Laissez-faire - market forces. Pluralists view. Marxist. Growth - maturity - decline. REFERENCES: Dash, Craig Hill, Moore.

INTRODUCTION Deconstruct the question — what questions need addressing?

1/ Industrial structure & change: what happening in 1960's -70's e.g. decentralise Data?. Exports?

2/ Explanation of change
 — Laissez-faire ⎫
 — Pluralist ⎬ better?
 — marxist ⎭

3/ Comparison with other sectors. National/inter.?

CONCLUSIONS Draw together.

Figure 2.1: Rough draft for planning essay

I find that for short essays a basic plan can be used on nearly every occasion. That is, we begin with an introduction, outlining the structure of the essay and defining some of the main terms or, if not defining them, pointing out that they are important and their meanings will be elaborated later. We then move on to *section 1* which puts one side of the argument, *section 2* which puts the other side and *section 3* which draws out the links between them. The conclusion makes brief reference to any general themes or conclusions which have come out of the essay. Armed with this basic plan and a method which allows me to set down all the points I think are relevant straight away, I find I can avoid that awful blank feeling of not knowing where to start and the panic, or even despair, which can follow. It gives me something to get on with and requires me to organise my thoughts. Even weak thoughts which try to answer the question are better than rambling accounts with little structure.

2.6 Using your own ideas

In writing academic essays you are expected to use your own ideas and yet not be out of touch with those of the various authorities in the field of study. You are expected to show your understanding of the matters under consideration by re-expressing arguments in your own words and perhaps by combining them in different ways. You should avoid using colloquial language since this is usually imprecise, for example, such phrases as *jumping the gun*, which we use in everyday language, might be better expressed in an essay by: *anticipating later arguments*. This does not mean you should continually be trying to use original thought; it is more simple than that. You are expected to show your own thinking about what various theorists have said by comparing their views and showing contrasts and similarities between them. Where to draw the fine line between being text-bound or pedestrian and being fanciful, undisciplined and idiosyncratic is something you will learn with experience. Your lecturers' comments will give you indications in this direction, and very likely, to begin with, you will get the impression that you have to stick very closely to the *official line*. Where this happens it is probably largely due to the fact that your present style of thinking and line of argument is rather different from that commonly held by authors who write in this field. Once you have learned the *discipline* of the approach, you will find that you have considerable room for manoeuvre.

2.7 Getting down to the writing itself

It is important to be able to break down the task of essay into a series of **component tasks** which can be tackled one at a time. If you try to tackle them all at once on a single afternoon or evening, you run the risk of frustration and feelings of inadequacy. It is important to recognise that writing is difficult and needs to be tackled in a determined and well thought out way. Below are the main stages of the physical task of writing; you will see that it should be regarded as a systematic task, and not an unplanned chore.

2.7.1 Stages of writing

Some time before starting to write your essay you should read the question and begin to think about it. Just having it floating about in the back of your mind for a while will help to clarify what it is asking you to do. Ask other students or your lecturer about it if you can.

Before sitting down to the writing itself, you also have to read the necessary handouts, your own lecture notes and published material, i.e., you have to complete some elementary literature research. Then you need to get your initial ideas down on paper (as mentioned earlier). This is a rather messy stage because you are simply trapping thoughts as they flit across your mind, and giving them some sort of permanence in the form of rough notes. To do this, you need to get plenty of paper and just write down any thoughts you have relating to the question, in any order, together with new questions that need to be posed, summaries of major issues and so on. If you are the type of person who finds it hard to write enough, this is a stage you need to devote more effort to. You need to be able to generate a lot more material than you will eventually use.

When you have **externalised** enough of your ideas, i.e. given them a preliminary existence by writing them down, you need to begin sifting through them, getting them into some organised form. Any kind of crude divisions which provide the basis of an attack on the question will do. Groping towards a suitable plan is often difficult and, when it emerges, it may seem so simple as hardly to justify the effort. But this is a very important stage, since it is at this point that your argument acquires its central coherence. Once you have decided on a simple plan, you can then go back through your notes, throwing out material you do not need and labelling the rest according to the section of the plan in which you intend to use them. If you tend to write too much, it is at the organising stage that you should make decisions as to how to limit yourself to what can be managed.

The final stage is to transfer your thoughts into a written argument which other people (i.e. your tutor) will be able to follow. This takes quite a lot of concentration in itself, so it is important that you do not try to collapse this stage into the two previous ones. If you do, you will tend to wander off at tangents, fail to express yourself clearly and very likely run out of ideas because you have been concentrating so hard on what you have been saying. It is at this stage that you *flesh out* your thoughts and illustrate your main points so that your meaning is as clear and unambiguous as you can make it. Again, if you tend to write too little, it is likely that you are not giving enough attention to the amount of explanation that a reader will need to grasp the full impact of your points.

It is at this final, presenting, stage that you bring to bear your armoury of **signposting techniques**: the use of linking words and phrases, such as *in contrast to, however, specifically, in comparison, a counter argument, following on from, thus,* etc, and the sectional structure as mentioned in 2.5.3. All of these things will help your reader keep track of your arguments.

Even when you have achieved a written version of your argument, you have not quite finished. It is very important to read through what you have written. (If you can, get someone else to read it too.) Make sure that what you have said actually answers the question set, and change sections which do not seem to work the way you intended them to. When you have edited and amended your work to your satisfaction, only then should you complete the final draft.

2.8 References and citations

One convention in academic writing is that you should always give full reference to others' work. The main purpose of this is to allow readers to go to the source themselves and make up their own minds whether or not they agree with our interpretation, and also to give credit to those who did the work in the first place. References can also give weight to an argument if an eminent authority is seen to be making the same point as you. You should never plagiarise – that is repeat others' words without giving them credit. Normally you will be caught out, but in any case it can distort your own line of thought. Furthermore, the language may be noticeably more complex than that which is desirable in a short assignment and the lecturer has no way of knowing whether or not you understand the point. If you use or refer to the work of others you should do so because it helps the point you wish to make, or because a point is made so well it bears repetition, for example it could be made with humour or particular clarity. You should also give references when stating **facts**. Your lecturer may ask you: '*Who says so?*' and would be quite justified to ask.

There are many ways to incorporate quotations into you essay, and you should use them only when they fulfil a useful purpose – not merely to affect a more learned style. You should always quote accurately and give the appropriate source. The following example is one typical method:

> 'The decline of many traditional industries, as for example spinning and weaving, has had a marked impact on the demographics of a region. Where no replacement industry has filled the gap, there has been extensive movement of labour away from the region; with a consequential reduction of public amenities and utilities.'
>
> (Marden 1992, p12)

Your assignment should be concluded with a reference section where full details of the publications you have referred to are listed. The names of the authors used in your assignment should be shown in alphabetical order; and you should follow the academic convention of differentiating between books and periodicals. The following example shows how the title of the book or periodical is identified:

MARDEN P. (1992) *Sunset Industries and Demographic Change.* Penguin.

SMITH J. (1993) 'The Closure of British Steel at Corby', *Economic Journal*, vol.83,pp.87-110.

2.9 Final assessment of the essay

After you have submitted your written work and received it back with the grade and comments, you may ask yourself **how** the work was assessed and **what the factors were** that your tutor was looking for. I have previously addressed this, in part, in section 2.4. However, for my example:

'Docklands decline was inevitable; what happened in the area in the 60s and 70s was a reflection of national and international economic trends.' Discuss.

I would be looking for the following points when assessing the final work:

70% or more

Assesses the *central changes* to the *economic and demographic factors* of docklands since *1960* – considers carefully what is meant by

16

the key words underlined and emphasises those changes since 1960. Identifies and discusses the *key factors* or *processes* that explain why these changes have occurred, carefully demonstrating the link between process and demographic change. Has discussed the *main agents* of change. Throughout the essay empirical detail (data) has been used to support arguments. The answer has indicated controversies in the literature that describe and explain these changes. A range of explanatory theoretical models have been drawn upon to give possible explanations, e.g. laissez faire/individualist, pluralist, and so forth.

60-69% inclusive

Describes the central *changes* to the *economic and demographics* of Docklands since *1960* – recognises the importance of the key words underlined. Uses empirical detail/evidence to support arguments, but has not considered it essential to bring out controversies in the literature on either the nature of the changes or their causes, or to adopt a well-supported argument of his/her own. Uses only material covered in lectures or in recommended reading. Has not made comparisons with theoretical models or alternative perspectives.

50-59% inclusive

Describes some of the recent changes to the human geography of Docklands. Is not precise in identifying the changes or in giving evidence that supports arguments. Has loosely related those changes to some of the factors or processes that may have caused them. Has emphasised the complexity of, or uncertainty about, what has occurred, or the reasons for the apparent changes. Has stuck closely to material given in lectures and some of the recommended reading – but has not gone beyond that information. The work of principal' authors has not been discussed nor has a concise argument of his/her own been advanced.

40-49% inclusive

Has written an essay on recent changes to Docklands. Made vague **unsubstantiated** statements about the changes. Thrown in now and then some sense that these changes are the result of some factors or processes, but generally does not link clearly the changes and processes. **Much anecdotal comment**. Gives very little evidence for assertions and restricts that evidence to what has been learnt in lectures and just some of the recommended reading. Has constructed a simple argument that has little or no logic and supporting evidence or has thrown in a variety of conflicting and poorly thought out ideas.

39% or less

Has written down almost anything about Docklands but does not attempt to structure it in any way. Jumps around between discussing the changes and the causes, not letting the reader understand the difference between them – suggesting that he/she does not understand them him/herself. There is little structure to an almost illegible answer. Makes unsupported statements and/or where any evidence is offered, sticks to what has been vaguely remembered from some of the lectures attended. Leaves the reader doubting whether anything has been learnt.

2.9.1 An example for discussion

As an individual or group exercise you might like to look at **Appendix 2** and, using the assessment criteria previously discussed, give the work an overall percentage mark. Compare your award with those of your fellow students. How did it compare? Do you have reasonable consensus? If not, perhaps this suggests that collectively you still do not have a clear understanding of what is required of an essay – a reread of this Guide might therefore be in-order.

3 Dissertations and projects

3.1 Introduction

I have deliberately used the title *dissertation and projects* because in many educational institutions the two are often regarded as the same thing. Your course, for example, may require you to complete an Honours Project in the final year. It is common on taught programmes, at both undergraduate and postgraduate levels, to be asked to undertake a major investigation. There may be educational purists who might argue that a *dissertation* is an independent study project carried out by you, on a subject of your own choice. Conversely, these same purists might argue that, a *project* is an investigation that could have a predictable outcome, e.g. a case study. For our purposes, I shall regard them as being the same: an investigation, carried out by you, probably on a topic of your own choice, requiring some **primary and secondary data** to be collected, followed by analysis and evaluation, the whole thing being approximately 10 000 to 15 000 words in length.

3.2 Selecting the topic

You will need to have a strong personal interest in your research topic to sustain sufficient interest over the subsequent weeks (or even years) of effort. When selecting your chosen field of work, ask yourself is it:

- ❏ feasible: e.g. can it be completed in the time available?
- ❏ useful: e.g. will it result in a useable model or method?
- ❏ balanced: e.g. a mix of quantitative and qualitative material.

To ensure your work is **feasible**, you should ask yourself:

- ❏ are the data available?
- ❏ do you have opportunity and time to pursue the research you are proposing?

- ☐ have you sufficient skill/knowledge needed – or the time to acquire them, e.g. understanding of statistical proving?
- ☐ will you need finance for travel, e.g. site surveys etc. and if so can you afford it?
- ☐ is there a sufficient body of knowledge that you can tap?

Additionally, by ensuring your work is **useful** (although this will be a value judgment), you will be better motivated if you believe in its usefulness.

In order to ensure that your work is balanced you should consider the possible outcomes of your work and the range of methods you intend to use to collect and analyse data. A piece of research that, for example, solely relies on questionnaires to collect data, will be less effective than that which uses a range of techniques. Will the end result of your work be conclusive or inconclusive? Both are equally valuable, for it may be that you had no intention to draw conclusive results, but rather to establish a methodology or model. It is important however that your work is not highly descriptive but balanced with sufficient analysis and evaluation.

3.3 Your proposal

Before you undertake your research, invariably you will be asked to submit an outline or proposal of your intended work. (Various names are given to this initial document, but I will refer to it as your **Proposal**.) Sometimes, your *Proposal* may be assessed and the marks contribute to your final grade. Consequently, in addition to being an important stage in the preparation and writing of your dissertation, your *Proposal* might gain you the additional marks to bring you up from a satisfactory pass to a very good pass. So due care and consideration on the preparation of your *Proposal* is vital.

Much the best way of starting to prepare your *Proposal* is to look at some previous students' work (usually included in the bound final-copy of the dissertation that will be held in the library). As a rough guide take note of those that have been accepted; look at their style and length. As a token example – and which one can be used as a basis for group discussion – I have included a *Proposal* as Appendix 3.

Your *Proposal* will need to:

- ❑ identify the area of study
- ❑ specify the objectives of the research
- ❑ summarise the more important pieces of previous research
- ❑ describe your intended methodology (of both research and analysis)

Additionally, I have always found it useful to include:

- ❑ importance of the subject
- ❑ assumptions underlying the research
- ❑ value of possible outcomes
- ❑ tentative timetable

3.3.1 What makes a good proposal?

Some of the things that stand out amongst other things include:

- ❑ the accuracy of the title
- ❑ the clarity of the aims
- ❑ familiarity with the current (relevant) literature
- ❑ whether the research methods and proposed work are clearly described
- ❑ whether the plan of work clearly reflects the aims
- ❑ whether the research can be done in the time available

Usually your *Proposal* will be returned to you after its submission with useful comments; these might include changes where it is felt you are being too ambitious and perhaps being too broad in your scope at the expense of depth of analysis.

3.4 Constructing a proposal

To assist me in explaining to you how to write a *Proposal*, I intend to use a theoretical example. The exact details of your own *Proposal* will, of course, be established by the type of investigation you intend to carry out. However, it is the developmental steps and the underlying process of writing a *Proposal* that can be discussed here using my example.

The route from initial idea for research to the submission of the final document can be illustrated schematically as Figure 3.1. The illustration shows the start of planning as the conceptual development stage.

At this stage you are thinking about a topic, talking to people and asking for advice, and so forth.

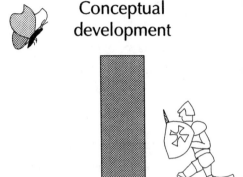

Conceptual development

From my experience, some people find this initial stage extremely difficult – they flit from one idea to another but never settle with confidence or for any length of time on a single topic; much like a butterfly landing on the head of one flower and then moving onto another. However, with appropriate discussion with tutors, by reviewing contemporary issues, and after highlighting personal interests, my experience suggests that this preliminary hurdle is quickly overcome.

Final written draft

Figure 3.1 From initial idea to completed work

It is a second type of person that is more problematic. This is the person who has missed vital early stages in the conceptual development of the project, and has already started to write up the main body of the research, possibly he or she has already sent out questionnaires, and feels that the conclusions are obvious. This type of person is depicted as the warrior in Figure 3.1., defending his or her position with great vigour; and seeing little point in developing a rationale for **why** particular methods have been chosen. From experience, I would suggest that it would be easier for this type of person to start afresh rather than try to justify their current position.

3.4.1 Hypothesis formulation

As an example for my hypothetical research project, I propose the following topic:

'In the U.K. tall people have a better chance to gain high rank.'

Whether you believe this statement to be true or false, or *how* I came to suggest this topic, does not matter for this exercise. However, it is this statement and idea or, as it is usually referred to, this **hypothesis** that I wish to explore in my research.

As previously stated, your research topic will undoubtedly be a subject of your personal preference and choice. How you came to your initial hypothesis, therefore, will probably be solely personal. We all have our own values and beliefs, and we each have varied experiences and backgrounds. Consequently, there are no rigid guidelines on how you should select your hypothesis. But you should ensure that whatever the area selected for investigation it has an adequate literature base, i.e. that there is already enough published material for you to work from, after all, you are not embarking upon your doctorate research and trying to discover new knowledge. So, carry out a small literature search (see section 3.6) to ensure adequate material is accessible.

Note that your final written dissertation may **not** result in firm conclusions. This somewhat inconclusive and unsatisfactory result may be due to a number of factors, e.g. lack of data. As a consequence, one of your recommendations could be that your work be taken-up by someone else at a later date and the research extended. Nevertheless, whilst it is not critical that adequate conclusions are reached, it **is** important that your **methodological framework** is acceptable. By this I mean that you have a well argued (and balanced) **approach** to your research, and that you have addressed all the important issues. Within this methodological framework it will then be possible for another person to expand your initial research, or continue it in the form of a longitudinal study, i.e. the data would be collected over a time period greater than you have available, so that changes over time can be measured.

3.4.2 Conceptual framework

The next stage in writing your *Proposal* is to think through the scope and extent of your work. What questions must you ask? What data must you collect? What analysis must be completed? This phase of your work is completed by deconstructing our hypothesis and planning the **conceptual framework**.

Figure 3.2 shows the process of developing the conceptual framework for my example. Based upon the original hypothesis: '*In the U.K. tall people have a better chance to gain high rank*', we look at the implications and ramifications of this statement. How can we prove or disprove our hypothesis? In essence, what we have to do is to *qualify* each segment of the hypothesis.

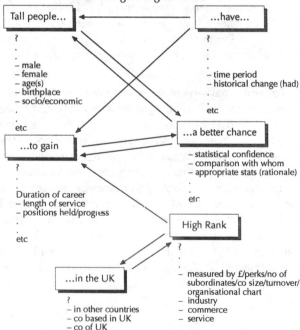

Figure 3.2 Conceptual framework for 'In the UK tall people have a better chance to gain high rank.'

Look at Figure 3.2 below and see how the hypothesis has been deconstructed to pose a number of questions. For example, what do we mean by the phrase *'tall people'*? Are we suggesting that our research is to investigate *all* persons resident in the UK? Clearly we need to clarify which UK residents our research is to encompass – and we need to say why (*the rationale*) we have selected this cross-section of the UK's population. Additionally, for the selected population under investigation, we need to define what the term *'tall'* means. Presumably we have access to anthropometric (i.e., human body dimensions) data that will allow us to identify above-average heights. Perhaps we could establish the term tall as 'those in the upper quartile' (i.e., the top twenty five percent of the population). Once again, we would have to argue the rationale for our method of selection.

The range of questions that the term *'tall people'* by itself generates can be lengthy. Our final selection of such people may be classified by gender, age, birthplace, socio/economic rank, profession, etc. Similarly, the term of *'have'* when used in, 'Tall people *have* a better chance...' needs definition. What historical time period are we referring to? Has there been a change over time, and is our hypothesis more valid now than, say, twenty years ago?

The term *'high rank'* used in our hypothesis is ambiguous and needs to be defined **within the context of the research**. Are we to measure it by salary, title, number of subordinates, etc., or a combination of these?

Only after this analytical process has been completed will you have a thorough understanding of the direction of your work. Its completion will result in a non-trivial paradigm, which is the simplification of a complex model. Moreover, it may have given you a greater insight into the complexity of the work you will be undertaking, and have established the rationale for the focus of your work.

The next stage of your research will be to establish specific objectives, and now that you have deconstructed your hypothesis, this part of your work is made far easier.

3.4.3 Outline objectives

Your *Proposal* is made up of your initial thoughts and plan of action. Consequently, you may discover that you need to modify, albeit slightly, your original ideas once you have begun your work in earnest. I say modify *'slightly'*, because if you veer dramatically from the original framework, you should be extremely careful that your work has not lost its original focus. The self-discipline required to keep within your original conceptual framework, even though you may be tempted to stray down an interesting line of discovery, is crucial if you are to meet deadlines and achieve a coherent conclusion.

Under the heading *Outline Objectives* you should give concise statements of a few (say 3 to 5) expected **outcomes** of the research: what you want to find out, NOT how you mean to do it. For example, rather than saying *'to do case studies'*, or *'to review the literature'*, or *'to send out questionnaires'*, express it as *'to establish X by means of case studies'*, or *'collect data by questionnaires to quantify theory N'*, or *'to compare Y and Z by means of a literature survey'*. From my experience and that of my colleagues, a frequent criticism is that some students propose a programme of work that would keep three people busy for five times the allotted time period – so do not let your ambitions become too expansive and grandiose.

By the time you have completed development of your conceptual framework you should have a fairly clear idea of your objectives and some kind of plan for attaining them. You should also have a much clearer idea of what literature needs reviewing and what statistical information needs compiling. Your *Proposal* should include clear evidence of **preparatory** background reading which does not mean that you have to do all the reading first in order to show the research is feasible. It is appreciated that these are early days and that further literature review will be done. Whilst you may wish to devote an *early chapter* solely to a literature review, note that you should be continually drawing upon authors' work **throughout** your text. A literature review is not a one-off exercise that once written-up in the second chapter, say, need never be referred to again. Quite the contrary, it should thread and weave continually through your reported findings for ongoing comparison.

An early draft of your *Proposal* should be discussed with your supervisor at the earliest possible date. Given the importance of this foundation stage in your research in identifying the scope, framework and focus of future activity. I would argue that this is the most critical part of your research. Contact with your supervisor, therefore, is vital.

3.5 Supervision

I am assuming that you have either sought a person yourself to guide you and be your mentor, or alternatively you have been allocated a specialist advisor. The actual advisor's title differs from institution to institution: advisor, director of studies, supervisor or research coordinator are common labels given to such people. What their responsibility is in various institutions, however, is less clear. But be sure of one thing, they are not *responsible* for you passing or failing. People who believe they have seen their supervisor regularly, and have heeded all the advice offered, are **not guaranteed** to pass. They will, however, have a greater probability of passing than those people who have little contact with their supervisor.

This being so, you need to find out early what your supervisor (or supervisors – you may have more than one) thinks that he or she is there for, and how he or she wishes the relationship to be conducted. The most likely source of difficulties will be your false expectations of what help your supervisor is going to give you; so try and establish his/her views and avoid disappointment.

You might feel a supervisor is too prescriptive on what you should be doing – which can be a danger if he or she has a special interest in the subject of the research. It is more likely, though, that you feel that your supervisor is being insufficiently positive, and you wish you were given explicit instructions (you may even come to make both criticisms at different stages of your research).

Your finished dissertation will show that **you** are capable of carrying out a complex and demanding task. So, do not project **your** own view of supervision onto your supervisor, but try to find out how he or she views **your** rôle, and in particular what level of initiative in the conduct of the relationship is expected from you.

3.6 Literature searching

You need to do a review of published material, to:

❐ find a subject worth investigating

❐ establish that your own idea is sufficiently challenging (adequate academic rigour)

- [ ] define the area you are working, and place it in context with related subjects
- [ ] read-around alternative methodologies
- [ ] develop new skills (e.g. planning/analysing questionnaires.)

With the information technology now available in most libraries, on-line searches and compilation of bibliographies becomes much easier. Consequently, you should think about which **keywords** concisely represent your area of research. Keywords are single words or phrases that the computer will cross-reference with its database. So, you will need an element of imagination in choosing you representative keywords, and discrimination in keeping or rejecting them. Go into the Library with your keywords and check the Subject Index for their Class Numbers. Check books that you know of in the Author Catalogue to see where the Library has put them. This gives you a test of your choice of keywords – if the keywords you have picked do not lead you to the books you have selected, then something is wrong. Finally, speak with the Librarian, as he or she will be pleased to advise you on sources of material.

3.6.1 Bibliography

Before you undertake your in-depth literature search, think how you intend to assimilate the material – how are you going to catalogue and reduce the information? Eventually, you will have to produce your own Bibliography, i.e., details of your source material. I would recommend you develop either a manual 'cardex' system or, even better, use a database or wordprocessor to store your material.

You will need to devise a standard procedure to assimilate the variety of texts you will meet: book, periodical, report, thesis, newspaper article, audio tape, video, etc. The two most common sources, book and periodical, should be recorded as:

For book	For periodical
❏ author	❏ author
❏ title	❏ title
❏ edition	❏ journal
❏ date	❏ volume
❏ publisher	❏ issue
❏ place, if non British	❏ year
	❏ page numbers

There are two relevant British Standards: *BS1629: 1989 References to Published Materials,* and *BS5605: 1990 Recommendations for Citing and Referencing Published Materials.*

To store this information on computer disk can be very useful once you are sufficiently confident with the technology. But, do not take the risk of having you hard-won data lost – always back-up your file; imagine the panic you will be in if you lose months of reading and notes.

When you come to turn your 'working' bibliography into its final form to go into the back of your dissertation, the entry format will change slightly. You will need to tie in the entries with your citations in the text. It is important that you refer to other peoples' work correctly, and conventions for bibliographical citations are dealt with below.

3.6.2 Bibliographical citations

There are two standard methods of making bibliographical citations within your text: **the numeric system** and **the Harvard system.**

In the numeric system every document you cite, i.e. book, periodical article etc, is given a number in sequence the first time you use it, and afterwards it is always referred to by that number. The number may be given as (16) [16] or [16] as you wish (so long as you always do it the same way). Your Bibliography will then list the publications in numerical order.

The Harvard system is to give the author's surname and the year of publication of the book/article referred to at each citation, and these are placed in brackets, e.g. (Jones 1991), unless you can work the author's name into your text, in which case only the date is bracketed, e.g. 'Jones (1991) describes this as...'

For the Harvard method your Bibliography lists all the references in alphabetical order.

Both the numerical and Harvard methods can become cumbersome when you quote excerpts from an authors text, when you must refer to specific pages: [16, p122] and (Jones 1991, p122). You should consider which of these two methods you feel more comfortable with. If you intend to support your arguments with footnotes at the base of the page (to expand upon or give additional explanation to a particular line of argument), then perhaps these will be better served by numerical derivation, leaving your main text using the Harvard system. Unless you are explicitly told which method to use, the choice is yours. Look at academic journals in your library and see how other academics write papers etc. (for example, the many Chartered institutions to be found in Britain maintain high scholarly standards).

If you refer to an author's work on more than one occasion on the same page, *ibid* should be used – which literally means 'as before'. If you have previously referred to an author, a page or so back, then *op cit* can be used. For an example page of an academic text where citations have been used, refer to **Appendix 4**.

3.7 Collecting data

Collecting and analysing data are very different operations, but you need to consider them **together** before you start your research in earnest. There is a state of mind that most researchers know of which is called '*information overload*'. This situation occurs when you collect more and more information, much of it highly irrelevant to the work you are doing. Often this state is caused by having insufficient pertinent data; sometimes it can be caused by '*data noise*', that is to say, too much information, much of it overlapping, much of it only cursory to your principal objective. Classifying your information will reduce this problem [see below for *classifying*].

A singularly important consideration in the collection of data is *access*. Will you need to use special facilities (e.g. computers), which may take time/money before they become available? If so, have you got it? Do you depend for access on permission which might be refused, e.g. the information is too sensitive or confidential, or people are too busy to see you. Consequently, to reduce the risk of your data being jeopardised, try to find more than one method of collecting information. Statistically, this will also give your results more credence -for example, people often lie in interviews and questionnaires, so alternative additional techniques of data elicitation will narrow the range of error.

When you record your data, do not concentrate solely on information you are personally interested in, as you may find after a time that some other factor is more important than you first realised. Going back over ground already covered will certainly be frustrating and may be impossible at a later stage, so it is better to research all the factors thoroughly first time around.

3.7.1 Classifying data

Classifying your data into a logical order will prevent future problems. An easy way of classifying your information is to draw up a list of topics on which you expect to get material and develop a filing system. Whether you adopt the system suggested here or invent your own system of classification, do not force your material to fit it – if the classification does not fit easily round the documents you are filing, then modify the classification.

Finally, will your intended methods of collecting or recording data require skills you do not at present have enough of? Try to acquire what you need early, and if possible practice in simulated conditions. Do not make your first interview, for instance, with the most important person on your list.

Field experiments in business studies will have affinities with interviewing. Some special problems in conducting interviews include factors such as: interviews are not easy to keep to a structure, they take place live, visual clues and non-verbal communications can be important, and you need to maintain some personal rapport with the subject.

3.8 Analysing the data

While you are gathering information from published material (secondary data) and collecting data from the field e.g. interviews and questionnaires (primary data), the experience can be very satisfying; often you may convince yourself that your research is going well because you are collecting so much information. Unfortunately this is not always the case, and you may be deluding yourself. Collecting data is an important stage, but it could be argued that an even more important stage is in the analysing of your data: this is what research is all about.

You have to analyse your data to show that you have:

☐ performed a novel piece of investigation (Note that you are not undertaking a PhD that would require you to complete an *original* piece of work.)

☐ worked independently

☐ attained an adequate academic standard

☐ used appropriate techniques

☐ made critical use of existing material

☐ placed your findings within the context of the wider field of knowledge.

How you achieve all these factors will, of course, depend upon the type of data and the nature of the area under investigation. However, your analysis may operate at a number of levels, namely:

☐ descriptive level; especially pointing out similarities, differences, analogies

☐ establishing regularities; discovering patterns, groupings, series and other associations

☐ causal explanation; correlation and regression, for example, might be used to quantify cause and effect

☐ prediction.

You will have to *defend* your technique and rationale, so you should be continually asking yourself: are there other ways of interpreting my data? There probably will be, perhaps too many to deal with exhaustively, so put the case for your own version against the stronger competitors, and disregard the weakest. Is there a simpler explanation than yours? If so, you will need to show why it should be mistrusted. You will need to make your case.

3.9 Structuring your dissertation or project

Your own institution may have definitive instructions on how you should present your published work; this is called 'house style'. It may instruct you on the line spacing, margins, page and section numbering, etc. If not, then the following convention should be used for the structure and presentation of your work (see Appendix 5 for an example of preliminary pages; whilst I have shown only the contents of the first chapter, it will give you a good idea of the layout):

- ☐ title page
- ☐ abstract
- ☐ acknowledgements
- ☐ declaration
- ☐ table of contents: chapters, appendices, tables, figures, illustrations
- ☐ introduction
- ☐ the main body of text
- ☐ conclusions (and future work)
- ☐ list of references quoted in the text
- ☐ bibliography, read for background information but not cited
- ☐ appendices, e.g. your questionnaire, organisational charts.

As a general rule, I would use single-sided sheets with double spacing for main text and single spacing for direct quotations. To allow for binding the left-hand margin should be 30 mm, and the right-hand margin 10 mm. Top and bottom margins should be 25 mm. Page numbering should in the centre at the bottom of the page for all pages including appendices.

3.9.1 Presentation

Your main concern must be with the content of your work. However, the way you present your material may affect the reader's interpretation and attitude towards your work. Consequently, ensure the finished product is professionally presented and that it **conforms to academic convention**. We will look at some of the more common conventions next.

The way I have numbered the sections in this book can be used as an example. Main section headings are largest, with sub-sections smaller, and sub-subheadings a smaller size again and bold:

1.0 Main heading

1.1 Sub-section

1.1.1 Sub-sub-section

I would advise you not to subordinate too far as this can confuse the reader – although sometimes it cannot be avoided if a range of peripheral topics needs to be addressed.

Also, note the method of numbering that I have used for **Figures** and **Tables**. A *figure* is a diagram, graph, illustration or some other form of schematic representation. Where, as an example, I was using the identifier of *Figure 1.2.*, I can deduce that this is the second figure used in chapter one. In the same way, *Table 1.2.* refers to the second table used in chapter one. All figures and tables must have an explanatory caption either above or below them. It is **of supreme importance** to always discuss your tables and figures in the text, highlighting to the readers what they should be discovering; do not leave it to the readers to deduce facts for themselves.

Short quotations – say, no more than three lines – should run in the text, longer ones should be set apart with indentations. Direct quotations should be inside single quotation marks (').

3.10   Language and style

First, it is not a requirement that your dissertation should be a distinguished piece of English prose, and possibly not every examiner would notice if one was. So do not feel inadequate if you think your style of writing sometimes lets you down. It is worthwhile, though, to take some trouble over making what you write as readable as possible. The most noticeable faults of poor writing are:

❐ loose structure

❐ unnecessary complexity

❐ restricted vocabulary

❐ convoluted phrasing

So, a good policy is to aim at the opposites of these faults: ordered ideas, clearly expressed, in varied language using simple phrasing. Generally, it is a good idea to use short words, sentences and paragraphs. However, whilst you should be looking for simpler ways of expressing yourself, you should be using the technical phrases – *jargon*, as it is known – that is used in your subject area for precision. Moreover, long sentences are less of a fault than convoluted and complicated ones. There is nothing wrong with a long sentence with a clear structure. But do not let any of these warnings impoverish your vocabulary, or restrict your use of analogy and metaphor, which can greatly enhance the readability of your text and the impact of your **own** ideas, and so improve your style.

Academic convention is to write in the third person in the past tense. It therefore reads as though you are reporting on an activity completed by someone else some time in recent history.

Probably no-one will read your dissertation aloud, but try the effect occasionally; it might tell you things about convoluted sentences or too many polysyllables that were not obvious on the page. Make judgements on the style, readability or otherwise of academic authors that you like, and try to see why they made that impression on you. Seek objective and critical comments from friends, family and colleagues. Finally, be prepared to edit, edit again, and again, until you feel it reads in a rhythmic manner. The hardest thing a researcher must do is to delete material, but it is always necessary to be brutal to ensure the writing is succinct and precise.

4 Management reports

4.1 Introduction

A report is a document of facts or findings, usually used as a basis for recommendations and actions. It should be written for a specific readership, although several people will probably read it. Additionally, and of particular importance, the report should be regarded as a source of information for the future, so it should also be a record for reference.

You may be asked to write a report as an assignment on your course, or you may have to complete a report for your employer when in industry as part of your sandwich placement. You will almost certainly be required to write reports once you are working.

A report may be the end result of many months of investigation. Consequently, it would be great pity if all your hard work was let down by confusing writing. If the readership is unclear about what you are recommending, or if there are errors and dubious conclusions, the credibility of your work will be put in jeopardy. Would you invest time and money in a recommendation that you did not fully understand?

Report writing can be identified as having six stages:
- establishing the purpose of the report
- thinking about the principal readers
- planning and setting key objectives
- sifting and organising the material
- deciding on style and structure
- writing, checking and reviewing

Many companies prefer their managers to use a particular style and layout (house style), but the main message of this chapter is still very relevant: the readership is, as always, the main concern of the writer.

4.2 Purpose

The *purpose* of your report may appear to be obvious: 'it is to give the reader the necessary information', you might tell me. I would agree with you in part, but go on to say that the major aim of writing your report will determine what type of report it will be. Basically, there are three types of report:

☐ **factual**: for example, to inform. You might have been asked to report on the performance of a type of machine, so the information included will be a straightforward statement of facts.

☐ **instructional**: for example, to explain a new procedure or method of working.

☐ **persuasive**: for example, to recommend a change of working methods; or to recommend the purchase of equipment to achieve operational cost saving.

Once the principal purpose has been determined, subsidiary aims can be identified. Thus, we inform in order to explain, and inform and explain in order to persuade. Clearly, the latter type of report is the most difficult to write as it has to motivate the reader(s) to **do** something – invariably to spend cash.

4.3 The reader

Your reader may have a completely different background to you, with little or no knowledge of the topic of your report. Conversely, he or she may be extremely knowledgeable. What do we know about him or her? Are you adopting the appropriate technical level, using the appropriate vocabulary? If we take time to find out about the reader(s), our report **can** be written in the appropriate way. So, get a clearer picture by asking three questions:

☐ What does the reader know of the subject area?

Two common mistakes in report writing are to either over estimate or under estimate a reader's knowledge, both of which can be very irritating for the reader. We must try to discover how much is known already so we can communicate at the appropriate level of knowledge.

❏ What are the reader's attitudes?

However good we think our ideas are, they may get thrown out if we do not take account of the reader's special interests, likes and dislikes. This does **not** mean that we give the readers exactly what he or she wants to hear – but we can couch our ideas in terms that he or she will respond more positively to. For example, if we know that the reader has made it well known that he or she is an advocate of automation and our recommendation is to use manual methods, how might we make our case? Possibly we could say that an automated system might be reviewed in the future, once the manual approach has identified what operational requirements are needed.

❏ What does the reader really want?

The reader is rarely a passive recipient of our report, who will accept all we say, and be totally swayed by our arguments. We need to know exactly what his or her hopes and expectations are of our report, then we shall know how to prepare our case accordingly. For example, if we know our principal reader is hoping for improved customer service so that sales increase, we should ensure that our **first** recommendation specifically addresses customer services and sale – even though **we** might consider our other recommendations of more importance.

You may think that it is difficult to answer these questions, especially when writing for a varied readership. In such cases, aim for the most important reader – the person who has responsibility for the project's implementation – but without offending others. Some people are only on the distribution list for courtesy, and they will probably only read the *summary* anyway.

4.4 Objectives

Having matched the purpose of our report to a specific readership, we must now consider what we want him or her to **think** and **do** next. Do we want something to happen? If so, how readily will our ideas be accepted? What problems might we encounter? In other words, what is the objective of our report? For example, it might be:

to persuade the managing director to authorise a proposed computer system for production control.

You should be aware of the words *to persuade* and *to authorise*. They indicate that we must produce a logical and solid case, one that will give our readership the confidence to accept our recommendations. So what problems must we overcome and how should we anticipate them? Say, as an example:

☐ **knowledge**: the managing director is a busy person, and his or her background is in marketing. We will need to supply ample background information and use layperson terminology.

☐ **attitudes**: we know that the MD dislikes spending on the production functions, so we must show what sales and marketing advantages could be gained from computerising the production control function.

☐ **wants**: he or she has mentioned in the past that out-sourcing in preference to in-house manufacturing should be strongly considered, so we will have to stress how computerisation will bring overall cost- savings, even if this emphasis overshadows other benefits.

Sometimes we can become embroiled in the information gathering stage and get too close to the information to realise that we have not considered the reader. All our hard work could be wasted because we have not satisfied the reader or dispelled any anxieties that he or she may have.

4.5 Organising the information

What the reader wants from a report is *easily-digested information*. We, on the other hand, sometimes want to show what an extensive investigation we have carried out, how far-ranging and complicated the issues are, what protracted calculations have been completed and how hard-working we have been. There is the obvious danger of *information-overload* for our readership, when really all that is needed is enough to help him or her to reach a decision. So, the **content** of our report must be organised and any superfluous material eliminated; which can be a difficult exercise when so much of your time has been invested in compiling the information. To help in this task, you must be continually asking yourself:

◻ how can I **simplify** what I am saying? Reject the irrelevant, exclude doubtful information and make sure you highlight the essential.

◻ have I **justified** my arguments and conclusions with facts that can be substantiated?

The facts themselves should therefore be a set of directions, which will guide your reader along a particular line of thinking. Once you have decided what information you want to include, the next stage is to think *how* you intend to **present** your thoughts and what **structure** would be best suited to your purpose.

4.6 Constructing a plan

Figure 4.1 on the next page shows how I have planned a report on *the use of a computer system for production control.* The best approach I always find is to use a large piece of A3 paper so that the whole plan of the report can be seen at once. I divide the page under major headings, and then decide what topics need to be included under each heading. I next decide which topics are most important, which are less important and which would be best located in the appendices. Lastly, I arrange the points in a logical sequence, so as to meet my objective. You might find it useful to write your sections on pieces of scrap paper and shift them around before deciding the best order.

A plan like this will show you what information you will need for *the body of the report,* what should go in the *appendices* and what is not wanted. Your plan will allow you to draw out *conclusions* and will be of great help in crystallising your *recommendations.* These four sections – the body of the report, conclusions, recommendations and the appendices, together with the *cover page* and *introduction* (dealt with in section 4.7.), constitute a typical management report.

Figure 4.1: Plan and structure

4.7 Writing and checking

In business you often find that organisations have their own house-style for presenting reports, but typically, a report is written with the following structure:

1.0 Title page

This should carry the title, date, author's name and position, and the distribution list. It may also carry a reference number or other classification (e.g. confidential). But do not overcrowd the page, a simple layout is always best.

2.0 Summary

This is a necessity if the report is long. It gives busy people a succinct, quick, overview of the report: it could include the objective of the work, key conclusions and recommendations.

3.0 Contents list

The contents of short reports may be shown on the title page – or not at all. Longer reports (say, more than ten pages) should always have a separate page, listing the section headings, sub-sections and appendices with associated page numbers.

4.0 Introduction

This should give the background of the report, and explain why it has been compiled. It usually states the objective or terms of reference (TOR) – this is a statement that identifies the **scope** of the investigation – who asked for it, any constraints that may prevail and special considerations.

5.0 Body of report

This contains your detailed facts and findings, shows how they were arrived at, and indicates the inferences to be drawn from them; all in accordance with your plan previously shown in Figure 4.1.

Make as much use as possible of charts and diagrams when discussing quantitative information, e.g. graphs, bar charts, pie-charts etc. A bar chart is shown in Figure 4.2. Note how easy it is to interpret the information from it, for example, if asked: 'Which option under consideration shown in Figure 4.2. gives the smallest operating cost?' I think you will agree that in this instance a picture does give the information in an easily digested way.

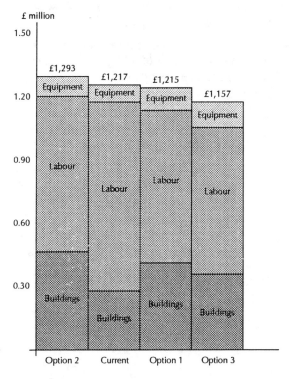

Schemes comparison: Breakdown of operating costs

Figure 4.2: Bar chart showing operating costs

The final task is to check for errors – especially spelling errors. You do not want to distract your reader, or cause the report's credibility to be placed in jeopardy due to minor errors. A professionally presented piece of work will gain the respect and trust of the readership.

A final point, before you distribute your report, is to always get a friend to read it. Ask if he or she fully understands the rationale of your recommendations and conclusions. Ask if the report 'stands alone', i.e., could anyone in the organisation /university get the **total** picture from the report, or do some sections require further verbal explanation?

The answer to this type of inquiry will tell you if the report needs further refining. Remember, one of the purposes of your report is to act as a record for the future. Weeks, months or even years may go by before the recommendations are implemented. Will there be sufficient data in the report and its appendices to allow someone other than you to understand what is required?

When you are fully satisfied that your report reads and looks professional you should spirex-bind it (if a large report, otherwise a single staple will suffice), and then distribute it.

5 Seminars and presentations

5.1 Introduction

You will undoubtedly, at some stage of your studies, be asked to give an oral presentation to your fellow students or to a group of tutors. It may be an individual effort or you may be one of a small group. The purpose of this activity is to give you the opportunity, in a controlled and supportive environment, to practice your verbal communication and presentation skills. As a future manager you will more than likely be in situations when you have to stand in front of small-to-medium sized groups of people (who you may not know personally) and give a presentation, e.g. selling your ideas to senior executives of your parent company. For this reason it is important that you understand some of the basic principles that can make your presentation informative, memorable, entertaining, thought-provoking and generally stimulating to your audience. Therefore, this chapter is to help you in the preparation of a one-off special event (although anyone involved in regular presentations, e.g. lecturing, could also benefit from reading it).

Three key areas need to be considered for the delivery of a successful presentation:

☐ setting objectives and planning

☐ structure and timing

☐ delivery

As always, it is the recipient, your audience in this case, that should be your major concern. Often we are preoccupied with over-anxious thoughts such as: *everyone will be looking at me* and *they all think my ideas are daft* or *I am sure I will be so embarrassed*. All such feelings are quite natural, but you must not let them dominate you. After all, it is the audience that should be of concern to you, not yourself.

Finally, if you know your material then this will give you natural confidence. If you do not understand it, however, you will find that your performance will be affected – the audience will suspect that your knowledge is superficial. Consequently, it is important that you are thoroughly prepared.

5.2 Setting objectives and drawing up a plan

The first question you need to ask yourself is: *What do I want to achieve?* The answer might be to sell a product, or make people change their ideas – to persuade, or to relay project details. What is the reason for your presentation? You have to set a *realistic objective*; you must be aware of what can be *achieved*. Consequently, you should be asking: *What can I achieve with this group?* So before you commence with detailed planning of your talk, first analyse the audience:

> how many people will be attending?
>
> what is their knowledge of your topic?
>
> what is their general interest: technical, organisational, etc?

It is very common for speakers to be too ambitious about the quantity of material they would like to cover and the level of knowledge of their audience. It is just as frustrating, although perhaps not as common, to hear a patronisingly shallow talk that is non-informative. Hence it is important that once you have decided what your presentation should achieve you should carefully plan its content.

By far the most useful way of planning your presentation is to use an A3 sized piece of paper with small scraps of paper to write your ideas on. First, write five headings on the A3 paper: *introduction, background, issues, proposals*, and *summary*. This will give you the basic framework for the key stages of your talk. Next, write on the scraps of paper the topics that you want to address. In the *introduction*, for example, you might want to give background information or a historical perspective. In this section you will also want to take time to explain the points you propose to address in the body of your talk.

As an example of planning, I have drawn up in **Figure 5.1** (on the following page) a rough draft for a presentation entitled: **Choosing a career in business management**. My audience will be university post-graduate students, and the time allotted is twenty minutes with ten minutes for questions and answers [I propose to tell them at the start of my talk that any questions should asked at the end]. My objective

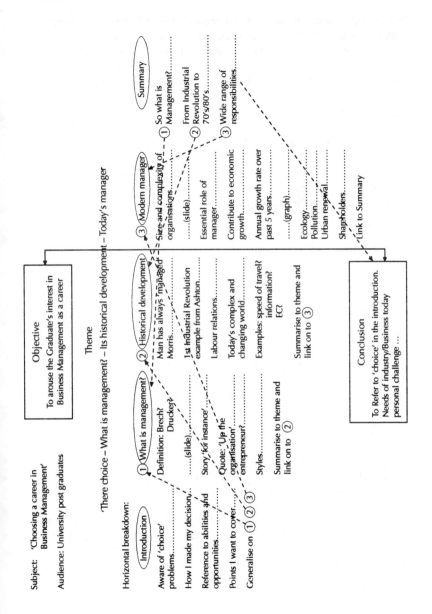

Figure 5.1. Draft plan of presentation

in this presentation is: *to arouse the graduates' interests in business management as a career.* To achieve this objective I propose to follow a logical sequence of, first explaining what the choices and opportunities are (my first heading on the A3 paper), next asking 'what is management?' (second heading), historical development (third heading), modern management demands (fourth heading) and finally, a summary to draw all the issues together.

5.2.1 Visual aids and span of attention

The visual sense plays a vital role in the learning and synthesis of new information. It is generally recognised that the breakdown of knowledge through the senses is roughly:

vision	75%
hearing	13%
feeling	6%
smelling	3%
tasting	3%

Thus, it is important that you use visual material to support and complement your information whenever appropriate. Additionally, it is also known that the concentration and span of attention of most healthy people is extremely small: only about 4 or 5 minutes. As a result, we must ensure that frequent changes in stimulus are incorporated into the presentation, i.e. verbal, visual, rhetorical questions and so forth.

If you intend to use acetates or slides as part of your visual aids, you should limit the number of words to *bullet-points* i.e. mention only the most important points, and restrict the text to 6-8 lines with only 6-7 words per line.

When using typed material the minimum size for the type is 5mm. For example, this size of lettering would **not** be acceptable. Look at the following examples; which size of text would be best suited to be used on a transparent acetate?

SLIDE ONE: THIS IS AN EXAMPLE OF TEXT THAT HAS BEEN
TYPED IN CAPITAL LETTERS. CAN YOU SEE A
PROBLEM WHEN USING CAPITALS? I THINK YOU
WILL AGREE THAT THE UNIFORMITY MAKES SEP-
ARATE WORDS DIFFICULT TO DISTINGUISH.

SLIDE TWO: In this example lower case lettering has been used.
This is better. However, the size is still a problem.
Beware of using italics or stylised lettering which can
be difficult to read from a distance.

SLIDE THREE: ## Much better

Even better

Always check your visual aids for correct spelling and other errors.
Get a friend to read what you have done, and accept any constructive
criticism he or she may make. Try and use colour to emphasise the
important facts, and whenever possible, use a picture or illustration,
e.g. static visuals such as large photographs, posters or charts all help
make the point for you.

Finally, remember not to stand in front of visuals when referring to
them; the use of a pointer, or simply standing to the side and pointing
with your finger, is quite adequate.

5.2.2 Checking and rehearsal

As a final check ask yourself these questions:

- are you confident that the content matches the objective?
- does the sequence seem logical?
- are there adequate links between themes?
- is timing sufficient?
- is the balance correct – weighting between speaking and visuals; weighting between sections?
- have you phrased your introduction correctly to set the scene?
- have you phrased the conclusion in words that hold people's attention, something that will stay in people's minds?
- does everything still work towards achieving the objective?

Carry out this check long enough before the presentation to give yourself time to do more work should any be needed.

5.3 Delivery

Some people can memorise their entire speech and still seem brilliantly spontaneous on the day, but this is a rare gift and most of us find that some sort of reference is needed. If you know your material well, your own visual aids may be sufficient to guide you through the sequence. However, there is a risk that valuable **links** might be forgotten. Therefore, it is advisable to use memory joggers: these may be words/phrases written on postcards or on a sheet of paper. Do not worry about taking a few seconds out of your oratory to read your notes; the audience may well like a little time to think about what you have previously said. Moreover, **silence** is a very useful thing to use: an important piece of information followed by a short silence can give great effect.

If you intend to use postcards or some other aid, do not read continuously from them. Your audience has come to listen to a presentation, not to watch you read from a script. Marking guidelines are in Appendix 6.

Your appearance gives a message to the audience even before your presentation starts, so make sure that you are appropriately dressed, i.e. conforming to conventional business standards. Body language must also be considered, for example, try and look around to all the members of the audience while you are talking – do not stare at one poor member who happens to be sitting in the front row. Do not wave your arms around or pace up and down. It helps too if you can smile occasionally. If you give the appearance of being calm and in control, this will give your listeners confidence in you and in your material.

Most of the questions you will be asked you will be able to answer easily. After all, you are the expert on your subject. However, if you cannot answer a particular question, do not try to bluff your way through it. It is far better to admit honestly that you have not considered that point and that you would need to think about it before answering.

If your presentation is a group one, plan beforehand exactly who does what. Try to avoid too much jumping up and down of different speakers – it is very distracting for your audience.

5.3.1 Getting ready

Ample preparation before giving your presentation will result in a smooth, professional event. Consequently, the following checklist should be followed:

☐ are you going to use a lectern? If so, make sure it is the right height for you.

☐ if the room is to be darkened, can you read your notes?

☐ will you be moving around? If so, are you going to carry your notes?

☐ is all the electrical equipment working, and do you know how to use it all?

☐ can everyone in the room see the screen?

☐ is the first visual aid ready to be used?

☐ do you need a microphone?

Finally, clear up behind you after your presentation so the next speaker(s) can prepare for their talk.

6 Research methods

6.1 Introduction

This chapter is to help you during your general preparation and planning of *research methods* that might be used when compiling information for the various types of coursework. '*I have got a fairly good idea of the topic that I want to investigate, my Proposal has indicated what I hope to achieve, but I am worried about what appropriate methods I should use, and when and how to use them*', is a comment often made to me. Others include '*Should I use a questionnaire? If so, how do I construct it, how many should I send, and what techniques should be used to analyse the results?*','*What are the best techniques to collect data for my particular topic?*', and '*I have read somewhere that I should construct an experimental design which shows that the appropriate research methods will be used. What does that mean?*' Clearly, therefore, research methodology is an area where many people seem to have difficulty. So, in addressing this issue I intend to guide those new to research, or to a particular research method, into part of the methodological literature, and to introduce some of the concepts they will meet. Students will discover that not only are there a great many books on research methods, there also seem to be a great many research methods. For simplicity, I have grouped the range of methods available into three:

surveys

observation

controlled experiments

This is intended simply as a convenient framework, and is not analytically rigorous nor all embracing. There are acceptable ways of doing research which may not fit comfortably within it, but probably most will have some affinities with at least one of these groups.

A research design which makes use of research methods from more than one group can be very powerful if the strengths of each method cover the others' weaknesses. It also widens your methodological experience, and looks good on your initial *Research Proposal*.

Before we look at the different strengths and weaknesses of the various methods, we need to understand some of the terms we will meet. First let us consider the relationship between these three terms:

theory

fact

hypothesis

6.1.1. Theory

In colloquial English, *theory* seems at times to be almost an antithesis of fact. To say something is *theoretical* is as brutally dismissive as calling it *academic*, and *theory* compared to *practice* or *fact* is always the loser. In reality, however, theory is not inferior to fact (i.e. **elementary data**); some theory is essential as a way of organising facts so that they make sense. A jumble of unorganised facts is no practical use, may even be psychologically threatening , and can only be coped with when we discern regularities and patterns. Theory can help us to spot these patterns.

Our forefathers had the theory that the Earth was flat; and for everyday usage it is perfectly satisfactory and makes excellent sense of the elementary data. That is why it lasted so long, until the contrary theory, that the Earth is round, was seen to make better sense of increasingly complex data. But most of us could get by perfectly well believing in the *flat-Earth theory*. What both theories have in common is the knowledge that we can travel to Australia, and beyond. We explain the data, that we can travel to far away places, by means of a theory – flat-Earth or round-Earth – which allows us to assume that travel to Australia can continue.

Another example might be the theory that anyone over the age of fifty has less opportunity to find a job than a person aged twenty. However, our theory is then placed on its head when we discover that in some Eastern cultures, the opposite is true.

In the first example, the *facts* of our travel allow us to establish a theory about the Earth. In the second example, facts derived in the UK for the over 50's underpin a theory about ageism and employment. But, as more facts accumulate, it becomes more difficult to uphold our theory. In both of these examples we have the same **two** intellectual processes at work. In the first, we start with facts and from these **generate a theory**; in the second we take an existing theory and apply facts to **test it**. The terms you will meet for these methods of operation are:

the **inductive** method of **generating** theories

and   the **deductive** method of **testing** theories.

6.1.2   Hypothesis

The difference between the terms *hypothesis* and *theory* and *fact* is tenuous, and could be said to be one of scale, and largely a matter of scientific convention. Generally, *theory* is used for a large assembly of inter-related propositions. *Hypothesis* is usually used to mean an individual proposition or small group of them, deriving from some larger theory (if it helps to remember the difference, the longer word is used for the smaller object). Thus in the flat-round-Earth example and ageism example, from each of the two main competing theories' were derived hypotheses to explain the behaviour of other planets and alternative cultures.

The *induction* method occurs when data are gathered, from which hypotheses are generated, and if the data can support enough plausible hypotheses these may in time be organised into a systematic *theory*. In *deduction* you start with an existing body of theory, derive hypotheses from it, and gather data to test the hypotheses. If the data supports or refutes the hypotheses, this tends to strengthen or cast doubt on the underlying theory.

Note the careful avoidance of words like *prove*. You can sometimes show that a hypothesis does not work, and too many such instances will discredit the theory from which the failed hypotheses were drawn. There may be other hypotheses you have not compared, perhaps that nobody has thought of yet, which would explain the data even better than yours does. The most you can claim is that your hypothesis gives the best explanation so far.

This is why one speaks of **testing** hypotheses, not **proving** them. To formulate a hypothesis, test it, and show it does not work is just as valid a contribution to knowledge as to produce one that does. Demolishing your **own** hypotheses may not seem very enjoyable, but getting a result you did not expect, and trying to find out why, could be a lot more fun than merely confirming what you thought all along. It could also be more fruitful; to test an idea, and discover its weaknesses with a view to improving it, is often possible even when supporting evidence is hard to come by. This leads us to two other important concepts we need to understand:

validity

reliability

'Research is valid when the conclusions are true ... It is reliable when the findings are repeatable.' (Sellitiz 1981, p26)

6.1.3 Reliability and validity

Let us look first at **reliability**. Your research design is reliable if you or someone else can repeat the research and get the same result, (this is why it is so important in writing-up research to describe not just the conclusions but the method, fully and precisely enough for others to try it if they wish). However, whilst reliable procedures should give consistent results over more than one trial, that does not make results true. Thus, we must now meet another term: **validity**. There are a number of ways of sub-dividing the concept of validity. The two terms most often met with are internal and external validity.

Internal validity is related to what was said earlier about the limits of proof, i.e. that you can only show that a hypothesis explains the data better than the alternative explanations. To do this you need to present the alternatives, and examine the merits and defects of them all. It may be, though, that there is a possible idea that you have overlooked. Or there may be defects in your treatment of those you have considered; you may have undervalued an opposing hypothesis, or been too generous to your own. If any of these things can be shown to have happened, your conclusions will fail the test of internal validity.

External validity, however, shows that the model has generic capabilities that allow it to address less precise data. We have already seen that for research to be considered reliable it has to be possible to replicate what has been done and get the same results. But there is the difficulty that the circumstances in which the original research was carried out might have altered by the time it is repeated, to such an extent that the second attempt cannot fairly be considered an accurate repetition of the first. If, however, the underlying concepts are the same, and the results correspond, then, as was said earlier, this has a bearing on the validity of the research; it shows that the conclusions which were drawn from the first study hold good in altered circumstances, and so can be **generalised**, thus proving external validity.

So, in summary we can say, a piece of research is **reliable** when it can be successfully **replicated**. It is internally valid when it correctly identifies the relevant factors and correctly determines the **relationships** between them. It is externally valid when its conclusions can be **generalised** to different circumstances.

6.2 Surveys

The survey is the classic method of business studies research. It is probably the most used in practice; and in many lay-people's minds the method is synonymous with market-researchers asking a battery of questions about product preferences. The method is popular with researchers (though not always with those being researched) because it can generate a large amount of data, usually statistical, from a lot of people. The quality of the data, however, is another matter.

A survey consists of asking people questions. A good survey is one where the researcher has thought of the right questions to ask and found the right people to put them to. But even a technically good survey may not be a good piece of research, because not every topic is amenable to the survey method. You first need to decide if yours is. Can you formulate a specific objective, frame effective questions, and find people who can give useful answers – and will they tell you the truth? Other considerations apart, people forget things, remember inaccurately, or make up answers rather than disappoint you by admitting they do not know. Additionally, the information you want may be obtainable in better/easier ways: it may be on record somewhere accessible; or you may be able to watch what people do instead of relying on what they say they do.

6.2.1 What are surveys good at?

My usual answer to this question is: as a *description*, finding out facts about a group of people – including opinions, attitudes, beliefs. But there is also a long tradition of using surveys in search of *explanation*, in order to discover causal relationships between facts – fluoride and tooth decay, and smoking and heart disease are two famous examples. *Descriptive* and *explanatory* surveys are not exclusive categories, and one survey may contain elements of both. A *descriptive* survey has to be representative of the population it purports to describe, while in an *explanatory* survey you need to control all the variables which could influence the causal relationships you are trying to identify.

Once you have decided that a survey will serve your purpose, and specified your problem in a way which allows you to frame your questions, you then need to identify your population. It may be obvious from the topic, i.e. *what do female managers think about under-representation at board-level?* So you survey female managers in the company. However, the issues are often complex, and some groups may be affected indirectly in ways not immediately apparent – overlooking these will leave the research incomplete.

After you have defined the population comes the task of identifying which individuals will comprise it, which may be much harder. You may have to settle for a *representative sample,* i.e. this may be a random selection or a defined group based upon, say, age. It is a very easy way of sampling, but the answers might be grossly misleading. For example, arguably opinion polls conducted by telephone, will be biassed towards people who could afford a 'phone. Likewise, interviewing commuters outside a railway station will tell you things about train travel and travellers, and nothing about the large segments of the population who rarely travel. You would do better to survey a group which represents the total population well enough for your findings from the sample to be generalised to that population.

6.2.2 Absolute certainty and probability

It is important to remember that once you have resorted to sampling you cannot attain *absolute certainty,* only *probability.* This is why it is desirable to use a sampling method based on *random sampling.* In sampling you are choosing a group to represent a larger population; *random sampling* aims to give every member of that population an equal chance of being selected, whether or not, as in our examples, they have a telephone or travel by train. The virtue of *random sampling* methods is that it is statistically possible to calculate the level of risk that the method you choose will give you, and whether your results could have occurred by chance.

6.2.3 How large a sample?

Two points should be considered when choosing a sampling method: *response rate* and *sample size*. For *response rate*, the higher the better, as this will give more accurate data and credibility to your work. A low or distorted response rate probably says more about your methods than about the survey population. If only a small proportion of your forms come back (if you were using a questionnaire) there is a danger that your sample will have become unrepresentative, in that some common factor will make particular groups of people more or less likely to reply.

Sample size can be too small to be useful, but it can also be unnecessarily large, in that above an optimum size it does not make the data much more reliable, and therefore does not justify the extra expense. There are precise statistical methods for establishing how large a sample needs to be to achieve a desired level of accuracy, and numerous text books are available which explain how to calculate it.

6.2.4 Questionnaires or interviews?

Questionnaires and *interviews* overlap in a number of ways: a questionnaire may be put to the respondent face to face, whilst an interview can be tightly structured round a strict schedule of questions. For simplicity, I shall refer to *interviews* as meaning a conversation where the questioner has some freedom in putting the questions, and the respondent has scope for extended answers. *Questionnaire*, I shall take as a set series of questions, not necessarily asked by an interviewer in person.

Choosing which method requires you to strike a balance between the sort of information you need, the people who will be supplying it, and your resources. Interviews allow you to follow up leads, ask for explanations, and get more detail, so the information you get, though less uniform, may be of better quality, and more reliable. Balanced against that, people' s reactions to the interviewer and the situation can affect their answers.

Questionnaires may be more convenient and less daunting to those who fill them in, and are certainly the cheaper way of putting questions to people, but they also have a notoriously poor response rate. Another disadvantage is that it is harder to make changes in a questionnaire once you have started to use it, if the early returns show up weaknesses or suggest new lines of enquiry. In fact, a questionnaire is not very likely to open up new areas to explore. The format tends to funnel the answers in pre-determined directions, which makes it easier to prove or disprove any hypotheses you start with than to discover fresh insights. Compared with the interview it offers breadth rather than depth.

In making your choice consider the implications, as discussed in the introduction to this chapter, of *reliability* and *validity*. It is usually considered that interviews are more valid than questionnaires, because of their greater flexibility in pursuing the important issues, but less reliable than at least the self-completed questionnaire, because of the risk of an interviewer introducing bias. The centrally important point is the quality of the data, which can be affected by the framing of the questions, i.e. their context and the way they are put, the circumstances in which the questioning takes place, or the personal characteristics of questioner and respondent.

6.2.5 Defining which facts are needed

After you have decided between questionnaires or interviews, open or closed questions, structured or unstructured interviews, and before you reach the detailing of the questions, comes *operationalising the concepts*. This is a critical stage, on which the success of the survey may depend. It means defining the area you are investigating in terms of facts which can be discovered, for example, to study the relative effects of differences in sex, age, race or class you need to define the categories in which you will place your subjects. Not all are equally easy – is age 59 middle-aged or elderly? Are your respondents middle or working class, and how do you know? But of most importance, will the questions you ask give you the **specific** facts you want?

6.2.6. Analysing the data

You should always **plan** your data collection and data analysis together, otherwise you might find yourself wishing you had done something differently when it is too late. Nowadays there is so much help available, at the analysis stage, from computer packages that you should make use of them whenever you can. Quality of output, however, depends first on the way you gather the data, then on how you process it. The computer will not find you a good sample, devise an appropriate questionnaire, make you into a good interviewer, or spot the silly answers. A poorly-designed survey with inferior data will not be saved by a statistics package.

When you have finished, if you have done everything properly, you will have a lot of data from a lot of people, obtained relatively quickly. It will be reliable, in relation to a much larger population than the group you studied; it will be in a form amenable to statistical analysis, so that it can be compared with data from other surveys. Against these advantages, you will have obtained your data in a very artificial situation – the more structured the questionnaire or interview schedule, the more artificial it will be. You will have people's answers to the questions you asked, which are those you decided beforehand were the most important and interesting ones. The answers they give will be what they want you to think is the truth – perhaps what they want to think. Deliberate lying, distortion or concealment are risks always present and hard to detect. Generally, a survey is a better method of obtaining facts than discovering opinions. The further it goes into subjective matters the more it is exposed to criticism. Cynically, it may be said that a survey only tells you how people answer survey questions.

So, whether you are devising a questionnaire or conducting a survey, think carefully about:

☐ why you are asking people questions

☐ why you are asking *these* people

☐ how you will analyse the answers.

6.3 Observation

Observation as a business studies research method requires you to observe, over a period of time, one or more subjects – which may be people, groups, organisations, events, situations, processes – in order to develop generalisations which you can then apply to the population from which the observed subjects were chosen. Time-lapse photography (memo-motion) is a technique that may be used to sample moments in time, e.g. vehicle movements or people into and out of a factory.

With any observation-based method, you need to make two decisions at the start: whether or not you, a₀ the observer, are to be a participant in the activity you are observing, and if so, how open you intend to be about the fact that you are carrying out research.

One element in the choice between participant and non-participant observation will be the setting in which the research takes place: whether it is a natural one for the people concerned to carry on the activities being studied. If people are placed in what is to them an artificial setting, e.g. an interview room – which is a natural setting for the researcher studying them – their relationship to the researcher and the research will not be the same as it would be in their normal environment. In this scenario the researcher will be able to take a detached role, and the research design can be highly structured, approaching the state of an experiment.

However, in a natural setting it may be very difficult for a researcher to be a detached non-participant spectator. In most circumstances of everyday life a passive onlooker, especially one taking notes, is embarrassingly conspicuous, and indeed might change the situation to an artificial one.

Two tasks which often give observers difficulty are **recording** the observations and **interpreting** the material in a way which gives useful results. Recording any observation-based research is likely to produce a great quantity of potential data if sufficient detail is recorded – your notes need to be full enough to remind you of everything important, even months afterwards.

Interpreting the material of observation is one of the harder tasks of this method. *Observation* is not just a matter of watching to see what happens; you have to try to make sense of it. You should look for similarities and differences, and try to explain them; watch for things you have already seen when they recur in new contexts; ask yourself why the same things keep happening. Then, look for exceptions, happenings which break your rules, and try to explain them – is your rule wrong or is the exceptional case really different in some way? To help yourself, you should devise categories into which you can classify what you see, until patterns begin to emerge from the accumulating evidence.

Observation has the advantage of enabling you to study a process in action, and it gives you time to build up a relaxed and natural relationship with the people you are observing. It is also easier to take note of non-verbal behaviour.

However, two major criticisms are made of all observation-based methods: first, they rely heavily on subjective impressions of particular cases, and so are not firm ground for generalising to other situations; second, the observer in a real-life situation – especially a participant – is in danger of becoming too involved and accepting the viewpoint of the people who are the subjects of the research instead of investigating them and the situation dispassionately.

The advantage of *observation* as a research method is that the material it yields is close to **reality**. As such, it is more accessible to its audience than the more readily organised data produced by more structured methods (e.g. questionnaires); it can hold its readers' attention, strike chords in their own experience, and make it easier for them to form their own judgement on the research. Other benefits are that it allows for a variety of interpretations, and it forms an archive of data which may be used by others for different purposes.

6.4 Controlled experimentation

An *experiment* is usually thought of by persons-in-the-street as the research method of scientists, and that it involves glass phials of chemicals, microscopes, etc., so *experimental* and *scientific* sometimes appear to be used as virtual synonyms.

However, *controlled experimentation*, especially in our business studies context, is taken in this book as something quite different. Rather than taking a passive and non-intrusive role as during *observation* and *surveys*, the researcher modifies the environment in some way and measures the effect of the change. For example, imagine we wanted to test different colour schemes in an office on workers' efficiency. A *controlled experiment* (changing the colour scheme for the office) could be set up and the results gauged. Another example might be the running of a computer model that has been designed to emulate a factory making toys. We could change a number of parameters in the model, e.g. machines' breakdown frequencies, to ask the '*what if?*'

questions. Hence, the *controlled experiment* can be a powerful method of discovery for business studies students.

The experimental method is based on certain assumptions:

> the real world actually exists, independently of whoever is looking at it;

> it operates according to fixed rules, in force at all times and places;

> if you know enough facts you can work out what those rules are.

To begin with, you need to *observe the world*, or the part of it you want to know about, and collect data on what actually happens. From this data you try to construct a hypothesis; an explanation that seems to make sense of what is going on. You may be satisfied with your explanation, but there could be others that seem to fit the data as well as yours does. Once satisfied that you have an understanding of the world under observation, you may then choose to develop an explanatory model (conceptual or computer-backed), alternative paradigms or theories. Then, instead of simply observing events, you could start to manipulate them, to alter some part of what happens, and see if other parts alter too, and if so in what ways and to what extent.

The reasoning is that if two sets of circumstances are identical, the outcome should be the same: if they are identical in every respect but one, and the outcome is different, the one point of difference must be connected in some way with that changed outcome. Note that the claim is not that the difference has **caused** the change: *correlation is not causality*. One piece of manipulation may demonstrate a link, but proving cause-and-effect is much harder work. Thus the *controlled experimental* method is a way of:

> testing a hypothesis derived from the data of observation by a process of planned manipulation under strict control.

Some of the complications that you might be confronted with will undoubtedly include links and causality (discussed earlier: see *internal validity* paragraph 6.1.3). If two items appear to be linked, either may be the other's cause, complete or partial. Moreover, they may both be effects of a third item; or it could simply be a coincidence. The degree of difference is also valuable information, and determining it could be a major object of your research. To achieve the necessary degree of control over your experimentation you need to isolate what you are studying from any outside intrusion which could affect the outcome of the changes you make. But this isolation brings difficulties of its own, in one of two ways: by isolating your area of study you have created an artificial environment, and it may in practice be impossible to achieve the necessary level of isolation anyway.

6.4.1 Methods of control

These problems are ones that you should be aware of when embarking on your business studies research, but do not let them deter you in conducting such experiments. Within the context of a business environment there are numerous applications that could result in valuable results. Your hypothesis might be that if you do something to people – retrain them, give financial rewards, introduce team working methods – it will make some difference, have some effect which would not have happened if you had left them alone. Thus, we are saying that the people are **subjects** and what you do to them is the **treatment** by applying different **variables**. Since you are applying the treatment to see if it stimulates a measurable response, the application or stimulus is termed the *independent variable*, the outcome or response is the *dependent variable*. We might, for example, want to see if the temperature changes in a cinema affect the sales of ice-cream; in this instance, the temperature (along with other factors, of course) would be the independent variable and sales of ice-cream the dependent variable.

If you gather your subjects, apply the treatment, and measure the outcome, it will not actually tell you much; you will do better if you know how they effect the dependent variable **before** the treatment as well as after, so you can see how much change there has been. Such a design, where you apply the treatment to all your subjects and measure the dependent variable you are interested in *before* and *after* the treatment, is called the **One Group Pretest-Post Test** design. It gives a measure of change over the time between the tests, within which period you applied the treatment; but probably quite a lot else happened to your subjects in that time, which you could not control and which might have affected the results. So, it could be argued that this approach does not give adequate *control* of the variables.

The standard experimental way of overcoming this problem is to have two groups, of which one receives the treatment and the other does not; these are termed the *experimental group* and the *control group* respectively. This design is entitled the *Pretest-Post Test Control Group*. The argument for this is that any extraneous factors influencing your subjects between tests will affect both groups comparably; the difference between the control group's pre and post tests will represent the effects of these factors; the difference between the experimental group's tests will show the effects of these factors **plus** the effect of the treatment. In sum therefore, the difference between the differences is the effect of the treatment – the only factor unique to the experimental group.

6.4.2 Grouping subjects

There are various ways of allotting your subjects to groups to achieve control. Two underlying principles, which can be used separately or in combination, are **matching** and **random assignment**.

With the *matching* technique you analyse the individual characteristics of your subjects which you think might affect the results of the treatment, and try to pair together people whose profiles closely resemble each other. Then you allot one of each pair to each group. By doing this you hope to ensure that any variable factor your subjects bring with them which might affect their response to the treatment is equally represented in each group; the technical term for this is **holding the other variables constant**. Clearly this involves a lot of work, but equivalence of groups is so important that it is probably worth it, provided you can identify the important parameters correctly and rate your subjects accurately.

By contrast, in **random assignment** subjects are assigned to their groups by some method depending entirely on chance. This might appear rather crude, but alternatively all the care and effort you take over matching could be wasted if you have overlooked one important variable. The great virtue of random assignment is that there are well-proven statistical techniques for establishing how likely it is to go wrong.

If your post-tests show a difference between control and experimental groups which you wish to claim as the result of the treatment, you may be mistaken; it could be a difference you accidentally built in when you assigned your subjects to their groups. But if you used random assignment, you or your statistical package can calculate a **probability level**, usually expressed in some such form as p =.05 or p =.01, which says that the probability of the difference occurring through chance is 5% or 1% respectively.

A point worth noting here is that random assignment is not the same thing as random sampling, though the underlying principle is the same. Sampling chooses from a population a group to be studied as representatives of that population; random sampling aims to give every member of that population an equal chance of being selected. You may perhaps use random sampling to assemble the subjects for your experiment. Then you need to assign them to their groups; random assignment gives every one an equal chance of being in either group.

So, by introducing a control group equivalent in composition to the experimental one, you have a design which is much stronger than the first one we looked at in its control of the variables. Now try to imagine how you are going to set up such arrangements in a real situation. In the business studies context you are more likely than not to be working with subjects who come to you, as it were, pre-packed, in established groups like school classes, work-teams, or hospital wards. Maybe neither you nor they have much choice in the matter; or they may be volunteers, so you have no choice.

6.5 Summary

In business studies research you are often confronted with quantitative as well as qualitative data, and both are extremely valid forms of information, but all data has little meaning unless it can be be used to support your argument. The only way you can interpret data is if it is placed within a **theoretical framework** so that you can explain its meaning. To give your research a focus, you must have a hypothesis to test. Whichever of the techniques of data collection you decide to use, it is of importance that you can defend it as **applicable**, i.e. it is appropriate for the work. If, for example, you are thinking about using a questionnaire, could you argue its advantages as compared with other techniques? If you are not sure, your data may be suspect. It would be better, therefore, to use various techniques and compare your results. Certainly this approach will indicate that you are aware of the problems that are waiting to befall an unsuspecting researcher.

Appendix 1: Further reading

This bibliography is to give you a start in looking for material in unfamiliar areas. The titles are arranged in roughly related groups, but there is some overlap.

General

BELL, J. (1987) *Doing your Research Project*. Open University Press.

BRITISH STANDARDS INSTITUTION (1978) *Recommendations for Citing Publications by Bibliographical References (BS 5605:1978)*.

BRITISH STANDARDS INSTITUTION (1979) *Recommendations for the Presentation of Thesis (BS 4821:1979)*.

BRYMAN, A. (1989) *Research Methods and Organisation Studies*. Unwin Hyman.

GILL, J. and JOHNSON, P. (1991) *Research Methods for Managers*. Paul Chapman.

MCNEIL, P. (1989) *Research Methods* Routledge.

WALFORD, A.J. (1980) *Guide to Reference Material*.

HOWARD, K. and SHARP, J.A. (1983) *Management of a Student Research Project*. Gower.

ADAIR, J. (1981) *Training for Communication*. Gower.

ARGYL, M. (1983) *Psychology of Interpersonal Behaviour*. 4th ed., Penguin.

BERGIN, F.J. (1981) *Practical Communication*. 2nd ed., Pitman.

CHAPPEL, R.T. and READ, W.L. (1984) *Business Communications*. 5th ed., Macdonald and Evans.

MARSHALL, L.A. and ROWLAND, F. (1983) *A Guide to Learning Independently*. Open University Press.

WELLS, G. (1986) *How to Communicate*. 2nd ed., McGraw-Hill

Theory and logic

BOLTON, N. (1977) *Concept Formation*. Pergamon.

DE BONO, E. (1976) *Teaching Thinking*. Temple Smith.

Writing

BAILEY, K.D. (1978) *Methods of social research.* Collier-Macmillan

BELL, J. (1987) *Doing your research project: a guide for first-time researchers in education and social science.* Open University

BENNETT, S. and BOWERS, D. (1977) *Introduction to multivariate techniques for social and behavioral Siences.* Macmillan.

BEST, J.W. (1970) *Research in education.* Prentice-Hall.

BLALOCK, H.M. (1982) *Introduction to social research.* Prentice-Hall 2nd edn

BRENNER, M. *etal* (1978) *The social contexts of method.* Croom Helm

BULMER, M. (1979) *Beginning research.* Open University.

BULMER, M. (1978) *Social policy research.* Macmillan.

BULMER, M. (1984) *Sociological research methods: an introduction.* Macmillan 2nd edn.

BURGESS, R.G. (1985) *Issues in educational research: qualitative methods.* Falmer P.

COHEN, L, and MANION, M. (1989) *Research methods in education.* Routledge 3rd edn.

DENZIN, N.K. (1978) *The research act: a theoretical introduction to sociological methods.* McGraw-Hill 2nd edn.

DIXON, B.R. *etal* (1987) *Handbook of social science research.* Oxford University Press

EVANS, K.M. (1978) *Planning small-scale research.* NFER.

GIDDENS, A. (1976) *New rules of sociological method: a positive critique of interpretative sociologies.* Hutchinson.

GLASER, B.G. and STRAUSS, A.L. (1967) *The discovery of grounded theory: strategies for qualitative research.* Weidenfeld.

HAKIM, C. (1987) *Research design.* Allen and Unwin.

HARRE, R. and SECORD, P.F. (1972) *The explanation of social behaviour.* Blackwell

HOWARD, K, and SHARP, J.A. (1983) *The management of a student research project.* Gower.

KATZER, J. (1982) *Evaluating information.* Random House 2nd edn.

KERLINGER, F.N. (1986) *Foundations of behavioral research.* CBS Publishing 3rd edn.

LANGLEY, P. (1987) *Doing social research: a guide to coursework.* Causeway Press.

LEEDY, P.D. (1985) *Practical research: planning and design.* Collier-Macmillan 3rd edn.

LIN, N. (1976) *Foundations of social research.* McGraw-Hill.

LOFLAND, J. (1971) *Analysing social settings.* Wadsworth.

LOVELL, K. and LAWSON, K.S. (1970) *Understanding research in education.* University Press.

McNEILL, P. (1989) *Research methods.* Routledge 2nd edn.

MANN, P.H. *Methods of social investigation.* Blackwell 2nd edn.

MILLER, P.M. and WILSON, M. (1983) *Dictionary of social science methods.* Wiley.

MOULY, G.J. (1978) *Educational research: the art and science of investigation.* Allyn and Bacon.

PHILLIPS, D.L. (1971) *Knowledge from what? Theories and methods in social research.* Rand McNally.

REX, J. (1974) *Approaches to sociology: an introduction to major trends in British sociology.* Routledge.

RILEY J. (1990) *Getting the most from your data: a handbook of practical ideas on how to analyse qualitative data.* Technical Educational Services.

ROSE, G. (1982) *Deciphering social research.* Macmillan.

ROSENTHAL, R. and ROSNOW, R.L. (1975) *Primer of methods for the behavioral sciences.* Wiley.

SAYER. A, (1984) *Method in social science: a realist approach.* Hutchinson.

SELLTIZ, C, etal (1986) *Research methods in social relations.* Holt 5th edn.

SHIPMAN, M.D. (1988) *The limitations of social research.* Longmans 3rd edn.

SILVERMAN, D. (1985) *Qualitative methodology and sociology.* Gower.

SIMON, J.L. (1978) *Basic research methods in social sciences.* Random House.

SMELSER, N.J. (1976) *Comparative methods in the social sciences.* Prentice-Hall.

SMITH, H. W. (1981) *Strategies of social research: the methodological imagination.* Prentice-Hall 2nd edn.

WARWICK, D.P. and OSHERSON, S. (1973) *Comparative research methods.* Prentice-Hall.

Survey methods

BACKSTROM, C.H. and HURSH, G.D. (1963) *Survey research.* Northwestern University Press.

BAINBRIDGE, W.S. (1989) *Survey research.* Wadsworth.

BATESON, N. (1984) *Data construction in social surveys.* Allen and Unwin.

BELSON, W.A. (1986) *Validity in survey research.* Gower.

BULMER, M. and WARWICK, D.P. (1983) *Social research in developing countries: surveys and censuses in the Third World.* Wiley.

FINK, A, and KOSECOFF, J. (1985) *How to conduct surveys: a step-by-step guide.* Sage.

FOWLER, F.J. (1988) *Survey research methods.* Sage.

GOYDER, G. (1987) *The silent minority.* Polity Press.

HOINVILLE, G. and JOWELL, R. (1978) *Survey research practice.* Heinemann.

JOLLIFFE, F.R. (1986) *Survey design and analysis.* Ellis Horwood.

MACLEAN, M. and GENN, H. (1979) *Methodological issues in social surveys.* Macmillan.

WARWICK, D.P. and LININGER, C. (1975) *The sample survey: theory and practice.* McGraw-Hill.

Sampling

COCHRAN, W. (1977) *Sampling techniques.* Wiley 3rd ed.

CONWAY, F. (1967) *Sampling.* Allen and Unwin.

SON, R.K. (1973) *Manual of sampling techniques.* Heinemann.

SUDMAN, S. (1976) *Applied sampling.* Academic Press.

Analysis

DAVIS, J.A. (1971) *Elementary survey analysis.* Prentice-Hall.

HELLEVIK, O. (1984) *Introduction to causal analysis: exploring survey data by crosstabulation.* Allen and Unwin.

HIRSCHI, T. and SELVIN, H. (1973) *Principles of survey analysis.* Free Press.

HYMAN, H.H. (1972) *Secondary analysis of sample surveys.* Wiley.

NORUSIS, N.J. (1987) *SPSS guide to data analysis for SPSS-X.* SPSS.

O'MUIRCHTEARTAIGH, C.A. (1977) *Analysis of survey data.* Wiley.

SILVEY, J. (1975) *Deciphering data: the analysis of social surveys.* Longman.

Interviewing

BRENNER, M. (1985) *The research interview.* Academic Press.

DOUGLAS, J.D. (1985) *Creative interviewing.* Sage.

GORDEN, R.L. (1975) *Interviewing: strategy, techniques and tactics.* Irwin.

McCROSSAN, L. (1984) *Handbook for interviewers: a manual of social survey practice and procedures on structured interviewing.* HMSO.

SMITH, J.M. (1972) *Interviewing in market and social research.* Routledge.

Questionnaires

BELSON, W.A. (1981) *The design and understanding of questions in the survey interview.* Gower.

CONVERSE, J. and PRESSER, S. (1986) *Survey questions: handcrafting the standard questionnaire.* Sage.

FREY, J.H. (1983) *Survey research by telephone.* Sage.

HENERSON, M.E. *etal* (1987) *How to measure attitudes.* Sage.

LAVRAKAS, P.J. *Telephone survey methods.* Sage.

OPPENHEIM, A.N. (1986) *Questionnaire design and attitude measurement.* Gower.

SUDMAN, S, and BRADBURN, M.B. (1982) *Asking questions: a practical guide to questionnaire design.* Jossey-Bass.

Controlled Experiments

CHRISTENSEN, L.B. (1980) *Experimental methodology.* Allyn and Bacon 2nd ed.

JOHN, J.A. (1977) *Experiments: design and analysis.* Griffin 2nd ed.

KAZDIN, A.E. (1982) *Single-case research designs.* Oxford University Press.

MYERS, J.L. (1979) *Fundamentals of experimental design.* Allyn and Bacon 3rd ed.

PILLINER, A. (1973) *Experiment in educational research.* Open University.

Appendix 2: Example of an essay

End of module assignment

'Docklands decline was inevitable; what happened in the area in the 60s and 70s was a reflection of national and international economic trends.' Discuss.

1.0 Introduction

The docks were the largest source of employment in docklands before their decline which started in the mid 1960s. In this essay I will be discussing the demand for, and the process of industrial decline of docklands from the mid 1960s. I shall be addressing the questions: what was the industrial structure of docklands in the 1960s and 1970s? and how and why did it change? Additionally, I will be identifying who gained and who lost as a result and what alternative policy solutions did the different interest groups advocate in response. In particular, I will be analysing if what happened in docklands was a reflection of national and international economic trends. During this period there was a strong drive of capital for technical change and industrial reorganisation, and I will assess the arguments that these factors were instrumental in the shedding of labour and the industrial crises. I will conclude by reviewing the debate over alternative explanations for industrial change. My discussion of the changes that have occurred in the industrial structure of docklands will be made by outlining the explanations and the policy proposals of the employers, the labour force and the politicians who were affecting and affected by the process of social change.

2.0 Industrial structure and change

This section discusses the decline of docklands manufacturing and transport industries, together with the alternative explanations.

2.1 Decentralising into the 1960s

The model of industrial change discussed in the article: 'The making and breaking of five industrial areas' (Moore *etal* 1973) divides their history into three phases – growth, maturity and decline. Employment in the East End (what is now the Borough of Tower Hamlets) peaked in the 1930s, when its traditional clothing, furniture, food, drink and tobacco industries accounted for 60 percent of manufacturing jobs (*ibid*). But at the same time many of the new 'growth' industries such as electrical engineering and motor manufacture expanded outside Tower Hamlets. They generally located on 'green field' sites beyond the built-up area of London (and around cities in the Midlands), where land was cheaper and larger sites were available for more modern mass production factories. For example, Ford's first car factory was started in the 1920s at Dagenham (beyond Newham) on a large flat site beside the Thames, with its own jetty for importing raw materials and exporting cars.

It was the older areas of heavy industry, in the North, in Wales, and in Scotland which bore the brunt of the slump in the early 1930s and suffered the most massive unemployment (Branson *etal* 1973). As a result these 'disaster areas' were seen to be a major national problem. The initial policy solution was to encourage workers and their families to migrate to the areas of greater job opportunities in the Midlands and the South East – but subsequently this policy was seen to be further impoverishing the depressed areas while leading to over congestion in the growth areas.

Laissez-faire views still dominated national policy in the industrial sphere, and there was strong opposition to the state intervening more deeply in the location of industry (Dennis 1978). But if the government could not tell private industry where to invest, might it not perhaps say where their investment should not go, i.e., the 'congested areas'? The civil servant in charge of 'depressed areas' in fact suggested that there should be an embargo on further factory building in the London area, and this led the government to set up a Royal Commission on the Distribution of the Industrial Population in 1933 (the findings of which were published in The Barlow Report).

The Barlow Report was overtaken by the outbreak of war but it formed the basis for the whole post-war urban and regional planning machinery, including both the decentralisation from London to the eight original new towns, and the associated policies for assistance to the depressed areas. In many ways the Barlow Report is a remarkable document. It was part of a trend towards rejection of *laissez-faire* views in planning. For instance, it argued that the movement of industry:

> 'has proceeded with little or no regard to the fact that it necessarily involves heavy expenditure by the community for the provision of such necessary facilities as new roads, housing accommodation, water supply, sewers, gas and electric mains, schools, churches, increased transport.... This expenditure, moreover, has to be undertaken at a time when facilities of a similar character are already available in the old industrial areas, where they must be maintained in spite of the fact that much of the labour in the new areas is drawn from the older ones, whose authorities, because of the loss of working population, become progressively less able to support the services for their remaining population.
> (Quoted in Branson and Heinemann, 1973, p.86)

Within East London the blitz helped to launch the policy of decentralisation, and rebuilding, with more space and green field sites and new towns outside the older congested areas which had been devastated by wartime bombing.

The County of London Plan, published in 1943, three years after the Barlow Report and inspired by it, foresaw the decentralisation of industry to new towns outside London. These policies continued into the 1970s, as can be seen, for example, in the *Strategic Plan for the South East* (1970) which, though only advisory, was the official regional policy. But in the late 1960s there were the beginnings of a 'U-turn'. In 1969 the working papers for the *Greater London Development Plan* (GLDP) questioned the desirability of further reductions in London's population and jobs (and hence rate base). But the policy of decentralisation had been so fundamental to post-war planning that it took a decade to halt. Even the modified version of the GLDP published in 1976 stated the desirability of keeping the commitment to decentralize jobs and people to new towns (Greater London Council, 1976, par. 4.23). However, there was growing recognition that East London constituted a large 'depressed area' within the relatively prosperous South East. Policies of 'decentralisation' came to be seen as part of 'the problem'. How important a part, compared to changes within industry, will be discussed subsequently.

2.2 Industrial structure in the 1960's

What was the industrial structure of docklands in the 1960s? The docks were employing some 23,000 dock workers, plus those in the associated lighterage (barge workers) industry in 1967 (Dash 1969). Apart from the docks, Tower Hamlets and Southwark were largely dominated by small-scale production. For example, in Tower Hamlets, in 1971, seventy-six percent of firms had less than ten employees and ninety-seven percent of the firms employed less than fifty workers (London Borough of Tower Hamlets, 1976). These small firms traditionally specialised in manufacturing industries catering for the vast consumer market of

London (e.g. clothing and furniture) or for the needs of the 'City', the central business area of London (e.g. the paper and printing industries).

Despite the dominance of small firms there were still large firms in manufacturing in the inner boroughs, although these represented a small proportion of total firms. The major large employers were in the food and drink industries, which had developed, like the clothing and furniture industries, to meet the needs of the vast consumer market of the capital city. In Tower Hamlets, the most important employers of this type were the breweries, which provided two thirds of the jobs in the food and drink industry (Shah 1974).

In the outer East London boroughs of Greenwich and Lewisham, as well as Newham, there were many large multi-national firms. Around three quarters of the people working in manufacturing in Lewisham, for example, worked in firms employing over 100 people (London Borough of Lewisham, 1976), while in Canning Town and the Lea Valley large firms dominated the employment market (Canning Town Development Project, 1975).

2.3 Industrial change and problems of interpreting facts

By the end of the 1960s (and considerably earlier in some parts of the inner areas) a two-fold process of change was under way. The old manufacturing and transport industries were declining whilst the service industries were expanding, but – and this is a very important qualification – not at the same rate. Manufacturing and transport jobs were disappearing far faster than service sector jobs were growing in the area, so that there were considerable net losses.

Overall, the docklands boroughs lost 82,750 jobs in manufacturing and 23,000 jobs in transport between 1961 and 1971, i.e., a loss of three percent per annum (*ibid*). Between 1971 and 1976 the rate of decline speeded up to four percent per annum, and by 1978-79 the rate of decline in Tower Hamlets was nearly double that. Over 65,000 jobs in manufacturing and transport were lost altogether in the five boroughs in the first half of the 1970s; the total number of jobs in these sectors was only just under 200,000 in 1976.

The increase in service sector jobs was not compensating for the decline in manufacturing and transport. In Tower Hamlets, for example, over 10,000 jobs were lost in the clothing, furniture and food and drink industries alone between 1961 and 1971, while a further 9,300 disappeared in the transport sector (London Borough of Tower Hamlets, 1976). Over the same period,only 4,640 jobs were created in the finance, insurance and banking sector. In the outer dockland boroughs the growth in the private service sector resulted in even fewer jobs, so there were net losses. If one compared the regions by means of the diagrammatic form of a pie, the 'pie' was not only changing its structure, it was also decreasing quite rapidly in size. If we take account of this, the patten looks like Figure 1.

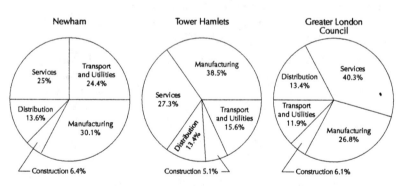

NB: The percentages in each pie diagram do not add up to 100 since there are some inadequately described jobs which are classified in an 'other jobs' category.

Source: Population Census, 1971

Figure 1: The changing structure of jobs

The decline in manufacturing jobs in docklands has been particularly severe compared to London as a whole. Twenty-five percent of the 335,000 jobs which left London between 1961 and 1971 were in the five docklands boroughs, although the area had only twenty percent of the total manufacturing jobs in Greater London.

One explanation offered was that docklands' traditional industries were those in decline, but in fact London's (and docklands' even faster) rate of decline was not due to the fact that the area had a particularly large share of declining industries. On the contrary, **if** London's manufacturing firms **followed the national pattern** there would have been a growth of some 13,000 jobs between 1961 and 1971 rather than a loss of 335,000 (Greater London Council, 1975, Table 2). So firms were choosing to close London plants as opposed to plants elsewhere and to move new factories to other areas. Why was this? Alternative conclusions are drawn in the next section.

These overall figures for docklands covered considerable differences between both areas and industries. Tower Hamlets had a particularly high rate of decline; this included the loss of nearly 6,000 jobs in the period 1971-76 in the small-scale clothing industry alone, together with huge losses in the docks (over 1 6,000 jobs disappeared in the transport sector as a whole between 1961 and 1976). Newham also suffered particularly serious losses – over 26,000 manufacturing jobs and over 13,000 transport jobs disappeared between 1961 and 1976. In Newham, however, the losses were concentrated in the largest firms as the article 'The making and breaking of five industrial areas' (*opcit*) has outlined.

Finally, although the employment structure of the dockland boroughs varied between the inner and outer areas, and the process of decline was uneven, it is clear that they were suffering from the same underlying trends; and the effects of these trends in each of the docklands boroughs was similar and obvious to anyone who looked around the area. Large numbers of derelict buildings littered the area. There were more and more vacant sites: 2.76 square miles in the dockland boroughs in 1971, and with further closures including the docks this must have risen to at least four square miles by 1981 (Docklands Joint Committee, 1975, p.35). The loss of industrial floor space led to a sharp decline in rate revenue raised from industry (in Newham the decline was 7.2 percent between 1966 and 1973, more than three times the national decline of 2.2 per cent). So the local authorities had less and less to spend upon the spiral of social problems which were associated with the area's industrial decline.

Tower Hamlets, where unemployment levels, already up to three times the national average in 1976 (6,154 unemployed in May 1976), rose by twenty percent between 1976 and 1978. The very rapid increase in unemployment in Lewisham and Greenwich (up by twenty-two percent between 1976 and 1978, despite a slower rate of industrial decline) indicated that there were groups especially vulnerable to unemployment (e.g. young black people who were particularly concentrated in parts of Lewisham). Both women and young people generally have also been hit by the employment crisis, with the number of women unemployed in docklands rising by fifty-three percent or five times faster than men between 1976 and 1978, and the number of sixteen- to eighteen year-olds unemployed rising by thirty per cent over the same time period.

In addition to the problem of unemployment there was the problem of falling incomes. Surveys of earnings have showed that manual workers' earnings in the service industries have been about a fifth less than in manufacturing industries (the majority of workers in the docklands boroughs were manual workers). So the loss of the area's industrial jobs meant a drop in wages for those who found alterative work. What is more, the average income in East London boroughs was already well below the Greater London figure (e.g. Tower Hamlets' incomes were thirteen per cent below those in Greater London in 1971/72 (Docklands Joint Committee, 1975).

In summary: despite local variations in employment structure the general picture in docklands was of rapid industrial decline leading to vacant and derelict land, a falling rate base or income for local authorities, and causing unemployment and falling incomes for the local population and workforce.

3.0 Explaining industrial change

While the fact that the docklands industrial economy was in decline was indisputable, different interest groups explained the decline in different ways. Massey (1985) was concerned with the fact that many small firms, such as those in the clothing industry, with limited capital and possibilities for mechanisation, responded to falling profitability by intensifying the labour process – precisely as they had done in the economic crises a hundred years earlier. In contrast the large firms, in the electrical engineering and electronics sector, for example, tended to restructure outside urban and traditional areas of the industry.

Some of the explanations which have been offered and the policies which were proposed by people specifically concerned with docklands, can be described under the headings of three perspectives:

- ❏ the individualist (*laissez-faire*) approach;
- ❏ the pluralist approach;
- ❏ the marxist approach.

The *laissez-faire* perspective particularly emphasises the role of market forces. According to this viewpoint the traditional industries were ceasing to be profitable in docklands. In itemising the causes for this decline of profitability, the major employers in docklands, who most clearly exemplified this approach, would often emphasize:

i)   The effects of technological change (e.g. containerisation) in response to the pressures to remain profitable.

ii) Changing market factors, e.g. competition from cheap imports as in the clothing industry or a change in tastes leading to a decline in demand for a particular product.

iii) Part of the explanation which was typically offered by those holding the *laissez-faire* view of events emphasises also the individual and collective responsibility of labour for the industrial decline of docklands. Labour had been too well organised, too militant, too greedy, too lazy, or simply too unskilled and incompetent to produce profits, so that employers had been forced to move elsewhere.

In contrast, **pluralist** tended to place **less** emphasis upon the inevitability of the effects of market forces and more on the social problems created by industrial decline. So they argued for the need to intervene via public planning policies,to strike some balance between the conflicting interests involved. In summary, they accepted that the employers' search for profitability, and the material and social needs of the existing working-class population, would not necessarily coincide in common policy solutions. The principal goal of the pluralist was, then, to find the compromise formula which achieved the most satisfactory balance between the conflicting claims (Dennis 1978).

In terms of explanation, therefore, the pluralist tended to play down explanations which implied that decline was inevitable and to emphasize those factors which contributed to the decline, which were the least affected by the market and the most amenable to public policy intervention. For example, the pluralist tend to stress the contribution to docklands' decline of the policy of decentralising from London. They would point to the negative role of local authorities who in the past had pushed out firms and jobs through planning policies such as clearing sites for housing and moving 'non-conforming' industry. They would emphasize the problems which firms faced in finding suitable premises (ibid).

The **marxist approach** tended to emphasize the key significance of market forces and the strategies required to maintain profitability. Whereas the laissez-faire approach took the market forces as a fixed and given element, the marxists, by contrast, started by challenging the very basis of the mixed economy/market structure. In common with the pluralist, the marxists emphasised the significance of conflict, but, in contrast to the pluralist view, marxists assumed that the fundamental conflicts of interest between capital and labour were irreconcilable. They also argued that local factors, such as inadequate industrial premises and transport, and local and central government planning policies, were very much secondary to these more basic market processes (Dash 1969).

Thus, while many policies suggested by the pluralist were also supported by the marxists (e.g. demands for councils to build factory premises), there was a fundamental difference in how particular factors (e.g. the importance of inadequate industrial premises) were fitted into an overall] explanation. Marxists tended to see such policies as short-term demands and part of a longer campaign to change the basic structure of society. Moreover, marxists emphasised the importance of local communities benefiting from industrial change and having some control over the process of change.

4.0 Conclusion

To blame the decline of the docks on the new technology of containerisation, or to conclude the inevitability due to national and international trends, fails to explain adequately why the port employers and shipping companies were keen to introduce the new technology. Moreover, such explanation leaves one unable to assess the alternative proposals for the future of the docks put forward by the different interest groups. For if decline was inevitable because of containerisation, there could be no alternative; and clearly, as identified from different theoretical approaches, alternatives **were** available.

The inevitability of docklands' decline as implied by the question, is therefore arguably unfounded. Whilst there was undoubtedly a national and international decline in the services of the port, this gave only a partial explanation for its rapid demise.

[3000 words]

References

BRANSON, N. and HEINEMANN, M. (1973) Britain in the nineteen thirties, London, Panther.

CANNING TOWN DEVELOPMENT PROJECT (1975) The aims of industry, CDP.

CANNING TOWN DEVELOPMENT PROJECT (1976) Canning Town's declining community income (Tate and Lyle case study), CDP.

CRAIG, G., MAYO, M. and SHARMAN, N. (1979) Jobs and community actions, London, Routledge & Kegan Paul.

DASH, J. (1969) Good morning, brothers, London, Lawrence & Wishart.

DENNIS, R. (1978) 'The decline of manufacturing in London 1966-74', *Urban Studies*, vol.15, pp.63-73.

DOCKLANDS JOINT COMMITTEE (April 1975) Work and industry in East London.

DOCKLANDS JOINT COMMITTEE (1975) A Strategy for docklands: setting the scene.

DOCKLANDS JOINT COMMITTEE (1976) London's docklands: a strategic plan

HILL, S. (1976) The dockers: class and tradition in London, Heinemann.

MOORE, B. and RHODES, J. (1973) 'Evaluating the effects of British regional policy', *Economic Journal*, vol. 83, pp. 87-110.

SHAH, S. (1974) The rag trade in London's East End, Runnymede Trust.

TOPHAM, T. (1973) 'The Attack on the Dockers', *Trade Union Register*.

WETHERITT, I. and JOHN, J. (1979) 'Office development and employment in greater London 1967-1976', GLC Research Memorandum 556.

WILSON, D. (1972) Dockers: the impact of industrial change, Collins.

Appendix 3: Dissertation proposal

The social psychology of clothing

John K. Smith

(Supervisor: Dr. J. Green)

1 Introduction

An understanding of why we prefer one type of garment in preference to another is comparatively little understood. Our relationship with material objects has been researched in the past (Rochberg-Halton 1968), but little attention has been given to the social psychology of clothing. The exception has been in the work of Dittmar (1992), who has included clothes in the symbiotic relationship we hold with material objects.

The conceptual idea is relatively simplistic: material objects are mainly there to use, but they also carry symbolic messages. Clothes are not just for keeping warm, or cars for going places. Symbols acquire agreed social meanings, and can therefore communicate information about the owners of objects, and contribute to their self images.

2 Method proposed

This work will closely follow the empirical framework established by Dittmar (*opcit*). However, the focus of the work will be clothing. Briefly, the approach will include the development and application of a questionnaire. A pilot study will be completed with 200 random respondents to validate the approach. Each will be asked to list five types of apparel that they consider important, and to describe why each was deemed important.

The work of Dittmar (*opcit*), identified that class differentiated the types of objects chosen: businessmen/women chose more antiques and sentimental things; the unemployed more basic things. There was a greater difference in the reasons given for the importance of objects: the businessmen/women were concerned with the intrinsic qualities of objects, and symbols of personal history, while the unemployed mentioned utility and leisure more. There were also substantial gender differences: men chose objects mostly for their use, especially for leisure; women emphasised sentimental possessions and those symbolising relations with other people.

In a second study (Jones 1980), businessmen, students and unemployed people were asked to list five objects which a typical member of each group, including their own, would list as important. It was found that there was some agreement about the objects chosen by any group, in the eyes of the other two groups. However, these stereotypes differed from actual choices in exaggerating the true differences between groups. For example, the **stereotyped** possessions of businessmen were expensive cars, filofaxes, business equipment and credit cards. It was thought they would have little time for photographs and other mementos. In fact the chosen objects in each group were more similar and less related to wealth or occupation.

A third study (Bloomer 1967) was about how material possessions influence the perception of others.

Whilst the design of the questionnaire, its subsequent completion and statistical evaluation are comparatively non-problematic, it is how far the results confirm or fit into any conceptual framework that is a crucial element of this work.

3 Conceptual framework

Social constructivism (McDowel 1967), the theory that groups develop and see the world through shared concepts and develop shared meanings for symbols (e.g. BMW owners) has been used to restrict and guide the scope of this work.

Theories about self and identity, that possessions (clothes) communicate information about the person to others, and contribute to the visible self-image, will be drawn upon (Slack 1967; Dittmar opcit).

Social identity theory (James 1960), is also invoked: the view that outgroups are devalued to sustain in-group self-esteem.

Whilst the time limitation imposed upon this work restricts the range and quantity of primary data to be studied, it is anticipated that one of the outcomes will be an **indication** of why particular clothes are purchased by particular persons. Specific objectives of this work are shown below.

4 Proposed objectives

1. Undertake a literature review to assess current debate and theory.

2. Discuss applicable espoused theories; and thereby construct a comparative framework to test the results from this research.

3. Develop a pilot questionnaire (based upon Dittmar's work); and extend the data set to 200 respondents.

4. Carry out quantitative and qualitative analyses on the information collected to test the original hypothesis.

References

BLOOMER, T. (1967) *Perceptions: the complete study*, Penguin.

ROCHBERG-HALTON, E. (1968) The *Social Psychology of Material Possessions*, Blacks & Heimen; New York.

DITTMAR, M.A. (1992) *Reflecting The Ideal Self*, Oxford University Press.

JAMES, P. (1960) *Social Identity Theory*, Pergamon Press.

JONES, R. (1980) *Who Am I?,Where Am I?*, Hollings Apparel Review, MMU

MCDOWEL, H. (1967) *Social Constructivism*, McGrett, Sydney.

SLACK, P. (1967) *Self-image Projection*, Heinmen.

Appendix 4: Using referencing and citations to support your writing

The following extract demonstrates the use of references and citations:

Employment in clothing manufacture in the UK has fallen from 423,000 in 1975 to 240,000 in 1990 (Werner, 1990). The sector runs a large and growing trade deficit that has grown from £1260 million in 1982 to £2120 in 1990 in real terms (ibid). It was argued that this deficit was initially the result of rapidly rising imports from low-cost labour in developing countries (Bowson 1989), but more recently from the EC, which now accounts for 52% imports (Jones 1990).

However, the industry has responded positively to the market challenge and by 1989 a strong revival had taken place. Output had largely recovered from the fall of the early 1980's, and in fact, between 1978 and 1988 productivity growth in the sector had outstripped the UK industry average (Wills op cit). Exports had also risen in real terms from £670 millions in 1978 to over £1506 millions in 1988.

The advent of quick-response philosophy (Barker 1989b), has left manufacturers and retailers searching for ways to improve their commercial relationship. Their goal is to improve the flexibility of the supply chain and to respond quickly to customer demands. Logistics and distribution, therefore, are key factors in maintaining a competitive advantage: 'Integrated logistics management is crucial to the turnaround of our industry.' (Christopher 1990, p16)

Other writers have argued that the combination of efficient supply management and marketing based upon strong branding are prerequuisites to the industry's existence:

> 'We simply can not compete with the wage rates from the emerging economies of the Pacific-rim, therefore .... we must identify what our trading strengths are and focus our business and markets accordingly. What we [the operational managers] must realise is that the customer demand must drive our business – not the other way around'
>
> (Johnson 1991, p4)

Appendix 5: Dissertation cover sheet and preliminary pages

Cover sheet (page i)

Modelling of a production-distribution
system for a toy manufacturer

John Simpson

An Independent Study Project submitted to the Bristol
Business School, The University of the West of England,
as part of assessment for BA(Hons) Business
Administration.

Date

Page ii

ABSTRACT

This work has included the use of a proprietary computer model entitled Scheduler to a toy manufacturer. The model quantified and isolated costs attributable to production-distribution for each product group in the company's range.

The affect of a number of product characteristics, e.g. size, weight, etc., were measured for varying levels of technology used for production-distribution. Direct comparison of results from the model between different departments in the company was possible; and by categorising the varying technology levels – ranging from manual to totally automated – used in each department it was possible to identify optimum systems.

The impact of production organisation and different philosophies of stock control have also been analysed to show their relative sensitivity to the total system cost. Consequently, the model has been used as a strategic planning tool to determine distribution system design.

Page iii

ACKNOWLEDGEMENTS

I would like to thank my supervisor Dr David Jones, for his continued support. He has provided much advice and guidance, especially at the critical early stages of my work.

Mr Steven Black, Production Director of New World Toys is thanked for his constructive comments and suggestions. I am indebted to all those people in the company – too numerous to name individually – who gave up their time to talk with me. The stimulating discussions held with operational management have been of immeasurable value.

Page iv

DECLARATION

No portion of the work referred to in this dissertation has been submitted in support of an application for another degree or qualification of this or any other university or other institution of learning.

Page v

CONTENTS

Appendix 6: Marking guidelines for presentations

Grade: 70% +

i) Stage management is excellent. Structure and logical ordering of the oral presentation is an exceptional standard; good use of language and technical terminology.

ii) Confident, well rehearsed, balanced, informative, good rapport with audience and entertaining. Good visual aids. Completed within the time allotted.

iii) The range of issues and problems portrayed in preliminary research clearly identified and discussed. Interesting. Accurate interpretation of any quantitative data presented.

iv) The major implications for the research, and important issues discovered so far explained and evaluated.

v) Clear conclusions drawn and clear predictions made on the basis of well defined methodology.

Grade: 60%-69%

Demonstrates good all-round competence in the basic requirements of a Distinction Grade but judged a merit because of a less cohesive presentation. Clear and lucid for much of the presentation, but flawed by, for example, poor visual aids, lack of affinity with audience, errors, omissions in key issues. Less decisive conclusions and overall a less confident argument than that of the Distinction grade.

Grade: 40%-59%

i) The logical structure and sequential line of argument is of varying quality. Predominance of descriptive material rather than a balance between analysis and descriptive material. Possibly: poor visual aids, poor eye contact with audience and constant reading of written material (*aide-memoire*). Has not grasped the importance of some issues highlighted in the research methodology lectures.

ii) Some conclusions unfounded/not previously argued through; predictions unclear or ambiguous.

iii) Standard of presentation varies in quality, and/or one or more serious omissions. Whilst the presentation has some excellent aspects, it is compromised in the overall assessment by periods which are unsatisfactory.

Grade: 30%-39%

None of the assessment criteria are fully satisfied, some may be so weak as to warrant less than 30%, but there is evidence that the student has made an effort in some areas of the presentation.

Grade: less than 29%

None or few of the assessment criteria are satisfied. There is little evidence that a proper attempt has been made in preparation of, or in the execution of the presentation. There are major omissions, misunderstandings, inadequate visual aids and the structure and overall presentation is unsatisfactory.